JOHN A. MACDONALD

CANADA'S FIRST PRIME MINISTER

M. RAOUL BOYER

JOHN A. MACDONALD: CANADA'S FIRST PRIME MINISTER
FIRST EDITION PUBLISHED IN 2021 BY YESTERDAY TODAY PUBLISHING
COPYRIGHT © M. RAOUL BOYER 2021

THE RIGHT OF M. RAOUL BOYER TO BE IDENTIFIED AS THE AUTHOR OF THE WORK HAS BEEN ASSERTED BY HIM IN ACCORDANCE WITH THE COPYRIGHT, DESIGNS, AND PATENTS ACT 1988.

ALL RIGHTS RESERVED. NO PART OF THIS PUBLICATION MAY BE REPRODUCED OR TRANSMITTED IN ANY FORM OR BY ANY MEANS WITHOUT PRIOR PERMISSION OF THE COPYRIGHT OWNER. ANY PERSON WHO DOES ANY UNAUTHORIZED ACT IN RELATION TO THIS PUBLICATION MAY BE LIABLE TO CRIMINAL PROSECUTION AND CIVIL CLAIMS FOR DAMAGES.

EDITING AND COVER DESIGN BY: BOTHBARRELSAUTHORSERVICES.COM

ISBNs:
978-0-9918558-5-8 (DIGITAL)
978-0-9918558-4-1 (PAPERBACK)

CONTACT THE AUTHOR: YESTERDAYTODAY5555@OUTLOOK.COM

INTRODUCTION

> "... I have fought the battle of Confederation, the battle of Union, the battle of the Dominion of Canada. I throw myself upon this country; I throw myself upon posterity; and I believe, and I know, that notwithstanding the many failings in my life, I shall have the voice of this country, and this House, rallying round me. And, Sir, if I am mistaken in that, I can confidently appeal to a higher court – to the court of my own conscience, and to the court of posterity. I leave it to this House with every confidence. I am equal to either fortune. I can see past the decision of the House, either for or against me; but whether it be for or against me, I know – and it is no vain boast for me to say so, for even my enemies will admit that I am no boaster – that there does not exist in this country a man who has given more of his time, more of his heart, more of his wealth, or more of his intellect and power, such as

Introduction

they may be, for the good of this Dominion of Canada."

— Sir John A. Macdonald, in a speech to the House of Commons. Monday, November 3, 1873.

John A. Macdonald, the architect of the Dominion of Canada, was an enigmatic individual whose pragmatism knew no bounds. From humble beginnings in Glasgow, Scotland to growing up in Kingston, Ontario to the halls of Parliament Hill, John A. Macdonald would create a legacy forged in the "wilderness" of British North America. He was beset with tragic personal loss, joined the militia to repel American invaders during the Rebellions of 1837, though never firing a shot, and then defended the leader of that invasion in a court of law. He rose from municipal politics to Premier of the colonial government of Canada West, and later, Prime Minister of Canada for nearly nineteen years. He also left a terrible legacy regarding the Indigenous citizens of this country, which still boils over to this day.

During Canada's formative first years, John A. Macdonald battled several attempts aimed at dissolving the union he had so wholeheartedly helped create. He battled the Fenians, fears of American invasion, Louis Riel, and rebellion in the west, which created the conditions for the creation of the North-West Mounted Police. He built a railway that spanned the entire nation, from coast to coast. He forged a National Policy that created a market for Canadian manufacturers and farmers, which had mixed results but set the stage for future battles.

John A. Macdonald won majority governments in more general elections than any other Canadian prime minister to this day. He made extensive use of patronage, in all its many forms. He rewarded his friends and political allies with great zeal and ruthlessness. George Brown, one of Macdonald's fiercest adversaries,

Introduction

once quipped that Macdonald's path was "studded with the gravestones of his slaughtered colleagues." A great conciliator, Macdonald, time after time, created consensus amongst the various factions in many of the issues facing the early years of this country. He faced financial difficulties many times throughout his life, flirting with bankruptcy more times than not. His health, always suspect, had to endure his chronic bouts of drunkenness, public and otherwise.

Depression and a suspected suicide attempt did little to mar his public image. His reputation was severely tarnished in future generations regarding his treatment of Indigenous peoples. His attempt to assimilate them reaped tragic consequences for several generations to come.

John A. Macdonald was the primary architect of Canada. It was not his goal. Indeed, it has been said that Sir John A. Macdonald disliked democracy; it reminded him of the American republic, which he totally abhorred. In this, the premier book of the *Prime Ministers of Canada Series,* we will delve into the private and public life of Canada's first prime minister. Little has been written about many of our prime ministers, and it is my hope to create a series through which you can learn the pertinent facts about our Canadian prime ministers in a short time.

CHAPTER 1
MACDONALD'S EARLY YEARS

John Alexander Macdonald was born on January 11, 1815 in Glasgow, Scotland as the third of five children. John Alexander's parents were Hugh and Helen Macdonald. Hugh was an unprosperous and ineffectual businessman who, by 1820, had had enough failures and bad luck to last most people a lifetime. Heavily in debt and weary of the struggle, Hugh packed up his wife and four children (the eldest, William, who was born in 1812, died of an unknown illness in infancy). They sailed from Greenock, Scotland aboard the *Earl of Buckinghamshire* on June 24, 1820, bound for Quebec City. After the forty-two-day voyage spent as passengers in steerage, the MacDonalds faced the more gruelling task of getting from Quebec City to their intended destination of Kingston, Ontario.

They travelled by flat-bottomed boats down the St. Lawrence River, through rapids and currents, and survived various incursions by many different types of wildlife into their camps. The Macdonalds then switched to wagons to get them to their destination. They finally reached Kingston on 13 August 1820. Immediately, they moved in with Helen's stepsister Anna and her husband, Lt. Colonel Donald Macpherson. Macpherson was a veteran officer of the American Revolution and the War of 1812, during which he had commanded Fort Kingston during the American invasion.

In 1820, the now-retired Macpherson, who was enjoying life as one of Kingston's social elites, gladly welcomed his sister's family into his home. The Macdonald family soon settled in, and before long, Hugh had managed to finagle enough loans using the Lt. Colonel's good name to open his first general goods store in Kingston. The store ultimately failed to thrive due to his lack of entrepreneurial skills. This pattern repeated itself a few more times over the next ten years, until finally Hugh gave up and settled into a job as a justice of the peace for Upper Canada's Midland District in 1830.

At one point in his life Sir John A. was overheard by his Private Secretary, Joseph Pope, that "I had no boyhood. From the age of fifteen I began to earn my own living." Little would change throughout his life; from about the age of fifteen John A. would be the sole provider for a great many members of his family. In the beginning his father had been a poor provider for many reasons. Later in life John A. would simply continue to take care of those whom he loved.

One event had a profound effect on Macdonald when he was seven years old. In 1822, he and his five-year-old brother, James Shaw Macdonald, were left in the care of an old soldier named Kennedy, who was an employee of his father's. While Mr. and Mrs. Macdonald were out one evening, Kennedy, an alleged alcoholic, took young John and James with him as he made the rounds to some of Kingston's less reputable drinking establishments.

After making the boys drink gin, then after a second failed attempt to have the boys drink alcohol, Macdonald decided to spirit himself and his younger brother away from the miscreant

Kennedy. While making haste for home, Kennedy caught up with the boys. He struck young James Shaw, who had fallen on the road, in the head with his cane. The resulting trauma caused the boy to experience convulsions.

A few hours later, John Shaw was dead. Hugh, even after being told the full story by John, failed to report the incident to the local police. Maybe he was embarrassed that he had allowed his friend and employee to kill his son. Either way, Kennedy had disappeared, and the incident was only referred to as an "unfortunate accident" in the Macdonald household. It was one that John A. Macdonald would never forget. Joseph Pope said, "The blow, the fright, and the liquor combined were too much for a child of his tender years."

In 1829, Macdonald transferred to the John Cruikshank Grammar School in Kingston. Hugh and Helen bore the tremendous cost of schooling Macdonald in order to improve his social standing. Yet, by the time Macdonald was fourteen, when most other children of prominent families were heading off to university, his family could not afford for him to go further down that path. Macdonald lamented this fact much later in life to his private secretary. John Pope recalled Macdonald stating, "If I had had a university education, I should probably have entered upon the path of literature and acquired distinction therein." Pope observed that, "He did not add, as he might have done, that the successful government of millions... the strengthening of an empire, the creation of a great dominion call for the possession and exercise of rarer qualities than are necessary to the achievement of literary fame."

CHAPTER 2
LEGAL CAREER

In the fall of 1829, a then fourteen-year-old John A. Macdonald travelled to the city of York (now Toronto) to write his entrance exam at the Law Society of Upper Canada. Passing this test would allow the young man to study law under a practicing lawyer. And pass he did. Upon returning to Kingston, Macdonald was placed under the tutelage of George Mackenzie by his father. He was given lodging with Mr. and Mrs. Mackenzie in Kingston.

For two years, Macdonald learned law from Mr. Mackenzie. He transcribed letters, did legal research, and performed discovery proceedings with clients. For more than two years, Macdonald applied himself with diligence in the trade his father had chosen for him. In 1832, George Mackenzie rewarded the young Macdonald (still a staggeringly youthful seventeen-year-old) with the title of branch manager of his Napanee office.

While in Napanee, Macdonald began to experience severe self-doubt. The young Macdonald became more introverted and began to withdraw publicly and privately. George Mackenzie, recognising Macdonald's struggles, wrote to the young lawyer, saying, "I do not think that you are so free and lively with the people as a young man eager for their good will should be. A dead-and-alive way with them never does." Macdonald misinterpreted the spirit of his mentor's communication and decided to become outgoing.

Along with two of his compatriots, Tom Ramsay and Donald Stuart, Macdonald began frequenting two local taverns. This was the beginning of a lifelong love of alcohol consumption. Macdonald strutted about Napanee as if he had owned it. Also, even though he had yet to be admitted to the bar and was thus prevented from trying cases in court, this did nothing to stop Macdonald from doing so, as would happen many times throughout his life, to stunning effect. In one such case, Macdonald defended a client who was accused of leaving a dead horse in the local Methodist Church. This was not a difficult task; Macdonald had admitted that he, too, was a participant in the misdeed. Macdonald stated, "It always taught me the weakness of circumstantial evidence."

In late 1833, Macdonald's cousin, Lowther Pennington Macpherson, also a lawyer, became sick with bronchitis and asked his cousin to run his practice in his absence. Lowther wished to travel to Britain to recuperate, as was the practice at the time. Macdonald agreed and was released from his agreement with George Mackenzie. He took up residence in Hallowell, Ontario (now named Picton, Ontario).

While in Hallowell, Macdonald began his general law practice with verve. Macdonald's willingness to push the envelope further than was necessary was in full evidence in Hallowell. Macdonald was the mastermind behind a plot to stop a local man from driving erratically through the streets with a horse and buggy. He and some friends placed a fence across the road; as expected, the driver hit it full-force one day while racing erratically through the streets of Hallowell. This time, after others were initially accused, Macdonald came forth and luckily was spared being charged by the magistrate because he was just beginning his law career. Macdonald had escaped again but was none the wiser for the experience.

In July of 1834, Dr. Frank Moore, a reformer who disliked conservatives as much as Orangemen, entered the Hopkins Hostel. Macdonald and a group of his friends were gathered outside the entrance. As Moore entered the building, Macdonald stuck an orange ribbon on the back of his coat. The doctor was furious, to which John A. profusely apologized.

Later that day, Dr. Moore spied the same group of men outside the hostel, laughing vigorously. Thinking they were laughing at him, Dr. Moore approached the group and began admonishing them and made aspersions regarding their Scottish heritage. The doctor attempted to strike MacDonald, who promptly knocked the good doctor to the ground. Macdonald began pummeling Moore, to the amusement of all who witnessed it. A local judge who happened upon the disturbance grabbed Macdonald to restrain him—but not before whispering, "Hit him again, John!"

In the court case of *The King vs. John A. Macdonald*, John A. was charged with assault against Dr. Frank Moore. Unsurprisingly, Macdonald was acquitted of all charges after a brief deliberation. However, the next day, Dr. Moore was found guilty of assault by a jury and ordered to pay a fine of six pence. Macdonald had escaped punishment again for his youthful transgressions.

In 1834, a cholera epidemic struck the Kingston area. As in the epidemic of 1832, the source was the incoming ships from abroad, which were docking in Quebec and Montreal. During both outbreaks, Macdonald had not been in the Kingston area. In 1832, he was in Napanee, and in 1834, he was sojourning in Hallowell. In 1834, an estimated twelve hundred people in Kingston died because of the Cholera epidemic, nearly one quarter of the town's population.

One of those who succumbed to cholera was Macdonald's mentor, George Mackenzie. This strain of cholera was particularly virulent; most recipients expired within twenty-four hours.

Mackenzie's fate fell within those parameters, and on August 24, 1834, George Mackenzie passed away, leaving behind a wife and an infant son. He was thirty-nine.

MacDonald felt the loss of Mackenzie keenly, but since he was never one to let an opportunity pass him by—a trait he exhibited many times in his lifetime—he began to solicit his former mentor's clients. He faced a quandary—to remain at his convalescing cousin's practice in Hallowell (Lowther, his cousin, would be dead by 1836) or strike out on his own. Still only twenty and yet to be admitted to the bar because of age, Macdonald decided to stay on at Lowther's office in Hallowell for the meantime.

By August of 1835, Macdonald opened his own law practice in Kingston. Never mind that it was another six months before he was admitted to the bar. Macdonald had successfully solicited many of George Mackenzie's former clients, and he also began to foster and perpetuate a reputation about town as a lawyer and a force to be reckoned with. To achieve this, Macdonald often took difficult cases, which most of his counterparts avoided. One such case was that of accused child rapist William Brass.

William Brass was a fur trader and merchant who, by 1835, had begun to imbibe with great vigour. Because of his drinking, his business had begun to fail. He hired lawyer Henry Smith to work on his behalf and straighten out his affairs. Smith promptly took advantage of Brass's drinking and wrested control of the man's property. During one of his drinking binges, Brass was accused of and charged with the rape of Mary Ann Dempsey in June 1837.

In September of the same year, Brass, who finally sobered up while in jail, began three separate lawsuits against Smith. The first was for fraud, the second was for damage therewith, and the third was for breaking and entering into Brass's residence. While these cases were proceeding, Brass hired lawyers Henry Cassady and John A. Macdonald to defend him on the rape charge.

The trial began in early October 1837. The prosecuting attorney was the newly appointed Solicitor General William Draper. After the alleged victim gave her testimony regarding the incident, Draper called two medical professionals and a midwife to the stand. All three agreed that the victim was raped. The crown's final witness was John Caswell, who stated that he had witnessed the assault but did not intervene because Brass was armed, and he feared for his life. Brass's lawyers, Macdonald and Cassady attempted to argue that Smith, Caswell, Mr. Stephen Acroid, and various unnamed neighbours of Brass had conspired to frame him for the rape of a young child with the express purpose of stealing his land.

Macdonald argued that Brass was drunk at the time of the incident, and as such, he was impotent due to his excessive alcohol consumption. John A. further argued that even if William Brass had committed the crime to which he was accused, surely, he was of diminished capacity and therefore not guilty as a matter of law. It took the jury slightly more than one hour to convict Brass of the charge. The magistrate set December 1 as the date of Brass's hanging.

Despite the protestations of many in the area and MacDonald's attempts to gain clemency and a new trial for Brass, the hanging was set to proceed on the appointed day. On that day, Brass and the hangman stood on the gallows in front of the

Kingston courthouse. In his final words to the throngs gathered, Brass again stated that he was innocent and that Smith, Caswell, and Acroid were the guilty parties. He asked those gathered if any or all of the three men were present, as he wished to gaze upon them one last time. Just as he finished making his statement, part of the gangway opened, and he was left dangling. Brass managed to kick open the remainder, and he fell, ironically enough, into the coffin below. The sheriff severed the noose from Brass's neck and promptly marched him back up to the platform again.

Emboldened, Brass yelled to the gathered assembly, "You see I am innocent; this gallows was not built for me. 'Tis for young Henry Smith." With a much shorter rope, Brass was promptly hanged—this time for good. Macdonald had lost the case, but he had given William Brass an ample and capable defence despite the outcome.

A mere six days later, the armed rebellions of 1837 began, led by William Lyon Mackenzie. Discontent with the Family Compact, a group of men who controlled the political, economic, judicial, and religious institutions in Upper Canada (in Lower Canada its corresponding oligarchy was called the Chateau Clique), caused people to rise up and demand radical change. The British regular military garrisoned in Toronto was sent to Quebec to help quell an insurrection there. Seizing the moment, King and his throng occupied an armoury on Yonge Street and then proceeded to march toward Montgomery's Tavern. King and his five hundred supporters took up position at the tavern. By this time, reinforcements from Hamilton arrived to bolster the regular forces, bringing their total to fifteen hundred. By the end of the day, King's forces, many of whom were unarmed, were scattered into the night after artillery shelling and a few volleys from the British regulars.

"I carried my musket in '37," was a favorite saying of Macdonald's in later life. As a member of the Sedentary Militia of Upper Canada, Macdonald was required to train for what was thought to be an invasion of revolutionary forces. Although they were not required, Macdonald stated, "The day was hot; my feet were blistered—I was but a weary boy—and I thought I should have dropped under the weight of the old flint musket, which galled my shoulder. But I managed to keep up with my companion, a grim old soldier who seemed impervious to fatigue." In fact, Macdonald never fired his weapon.

Even though Mackenzie's rebellion fizzled out on Yonge Street, some Americans felt that the good citizens of Canada still needed liberating. One such group was the Hunters' Lodge, a clandestine organization of between forty thousand and eighty thousand people in Vermont, upstate New York, and the Great Lakes region. What began as a group of exiled rebels from Canada grew into something much greater. Americans who felt that "radical republicanism," in conjunction with the ending of the power of the British aristocracy in North America, devised a plan to invade Canada. John W. Birge, the commander of the small army assembling to invade Canada, stated in a proclamation intended for the hungry republican masses across the border, "We have come to your rescue. We have heard the groans of your distress and have seen the tears of anguish burning on the cheeks of your exiled companions. They have besought us to aid them and you in the great work of reform, and to establish on your own native soil, EQUAL RIGHTS and EQUAL PRIVILEGES."

Birge decided that the town of Prescott, downriver from Kingston on the St. Lawrence River, would be their entry point. Despite suffering from previous military defeats up to this point, and the fact that Prescott was the site of Fort Wellington, the group of three hundred and fifty men embarked across the river in three ships on November 12, 1838. Once across the river, "Major

General" Birge, under the pretence of a stomach ailment, made haste back across the river to safety with about two hundred of the original force. The promised reinforcements never arrived. This left his second-in-command, Nils von Schoultz, a Polish veteran, in charge of what remained of the invading force.

Born in Finland in 1807, von Schoultz was trained by the Swedish and fought against the Russians in Poland in 1831. Having been captured, von Schoultz managed to escape and made his way to France, where he joined the Foreign Legion. After fighting in Africa under the French flag, he deserted and went to Italy, where he met his Scottish wife. After a brief sojourn in Sweden, Scotland, and England, von Schoultz left behind his wife and family and settled in upstate New York. It was there that he put his chemistry education to good use and devised a method to extract salt from brine. It was against this backdrop that von Schoultz was recruited to the Hunters Lodge by John W. Birge. He felt that Canada's subjugation at the hands of the British "devil" needed to be dealt with decisively. So, on November 11, von Schoultz left Ogdensburg, New York aboard the *Charlotte of Toronto*, bound for Prescott, Ontario.

Because of British infiltration into the Hunters' Lodge, news of the invasion came as little surprise to the British at Fort Wellington or at Kingston. As a result, the invading patriots had to make landfall east of Prescott, which did not bode well for the invasion force. With their commander and two hundred others in the wind heading back to the United States, command fell to von Schoultz. After surveying the situation, he decided to mount a defence using a stone windmill as his base of operations. After two assaults by British regulars and five days of siege, von Schoultz decided to surrender unconditionally. The invaders had suffered fifty-three dead and sixty wounded, while another one hundred and fifty were taken prisoner. The British suffered seventeen killed and sixty wounded. One of the British soldiers found near the windmill was mercilessly decapitated during the battle. This act had repercussions in the upcoming trials.

In the aftermath of the invasion, the one hundred and fifty invaders captured by the British were forced to walk from Prescott to Fort Henry in Kingston, by way of Main Street, Kingston. It was during that forced march that von Schoultz realized that he had been deceived by his American friends. Canadians were not in such bad straits after all. As the trials of the eleven deemed to be the ringleaders of the ill-fated invasion began, a Kingston resident whose brother was one of those eleven asked Macdonald to represent his brother. He wanted to ensure a fair trial. Since the proceedings were actually court martials and not in civilian court, all Macdonald could do was observe and consult with his client. The accused had to speak for themselves.

After the trial of that man, Macdonald was approached by von Schoultz, who wanted Macdonald to advise him also. Macdonald agreed, but despite his advice, von Schoultz accepted responsibility and pled guilty. All that Macdonald could do for the man now was attempt to have him executed by firing squad, as opposed to hanging. In this matter, Macdonald was unsuccessful. Nils von Schultz and the eleven other invaders were hanged on December 8, 1838.

The von Schoultz trial was an important turning point in Macdonald's life. Although this was the second of his clients to be found guilty, and he had failed to fight in the rebellions, and despite his refusal of a promotion during the same rebellion, Macdonald was making quite a reputation for himself. Despite protestations from the conservative elite in Kingston, Macdonald also successfully defended eight rebels from the botched invasion who were duped, due to their illiterate nature, into signing affidavits of guilt in the affair. What the miscreants did not realize was that they were signing their own death warrants. Stating that the whole affair was "an outrage to the administration of justice," Macdonald was able to get the men's convictions overturned, thus allowing them to go free.

Also, the invasion by American rebels solidified in Macdonald the burning desire to protect British North America from the republican hordes to the South. The American Civil War created the perfect climate for this to happen twenty-five years later.

Macdonald was also able to successfully prosecute Colonel Dundas of the 83rd Regiment for the libel of John Ashley, who was the jailer in Kingston. Dundas had accused him of facilitating the escapes of fifteen rebel prisoners from the jail. Macdonald was able to win a judgement of two hundred pounds for his client. At a mere twenty-three years of age Macdonald defeated Attorney General Christopher Hagerman. Macdonald's star was most certainly rising.

In the fall of 1841, Macdonald's father, Hugh, died of a cerebral hemorrhage at the age of fifty-four. Within a short time, John A. became sick himself with a stomach ailment. Always of precarious health, Macdonald often spent days in bed, with a plethora of books as company. His doctors suggested that he take several weeks of rest, and John A. decided to travel to England. Just prior to leaving, Macdonald engaged himself in a three-day game of cards and secured four hundred pounds as winnings.

While in England, Macdonald spent money as if it grew on trees, a habit which brought him to the brink of bankruptcy many times. He purchased items for his beloved mother and sisters. He travelled throughout the British Isles, enjoying himself to the fullest. He drank, he courted, enjoyed the theatre, visited museums, and before long, his intended one month of rest became two months. It was during this time that he met his future wife, Isabella, his first cousin on his mother's side of the family.

Isabella, six years Macdonald's senior, was a demure lady of average intelligence, with large and beautiful blue eyes. With a "sweet gentleness of manner and tender sympathetic nature," Isabella also possessed an internal fortitude second to none. And with Macdonald as her eventual husband, she would need it.

CHAPTER 3
EVOLUTION OF THE POLITICIAN

Before Isabella and John A. married on September 1, 1842, Macdonald sought to elevate himself in the public's eye even more by declaring himself a candidate for alderman in the Fourth Ward in Kingston's municipal election, which was due to take place in 1843. John A. craved power and status, and this election would help him achieve both. By a margin of 156 to 43, Macdonald defeated his opponent, Colonel Jackson, for a seat on the town council.

In November 1843, it was decided to move the capital of the Province of Canada from Kingston to Montreal. This decision had profound effects on the economic fortunes of Kingston and its citizens, particularly Macdonald. A building boom had been occurring for many years, and even Macdonald had invested heavily in real estate during the preceding years. In March of 1844, Macdonald was approached by several citizens asking that he consider vying for a seat in the legislature as the conservative candidate for Kingston. After a petition of 225 names was presented to him, he gladly accepted. In appreciation, he told his followers in a brief written statement, "I, therefore, need scarcely state my firm belief that the prosperity of Canada depends upon its permanent connection with the Mother Country, and that I shall resist to the utmost any attempt (from whatever quarter it may come) which may tend to weaken that union. "When asked years later by his personal secretary, Joseph Pope, how he came to be the candidate in the 1844 election, Macdonald slyly stated, "To fill a gap. There seemed to be no one else available, so I was pitched upon."

In the October 1844 election, Macdonald swept to victory by a margin of 244 to 42 over his opponent, Anthony Manahan. This was achieved in no small part by supplying alcohol to the voters, usually through the local taverns at the candidate's expense. On November 28, Macdonald entered parliament as a backbencher. He took his time in getting the lay of the land in more ways than one. While Macdonald was in Montreal attending the first session of Parliament, one observer described Macdonald's appearance as follows: "His face was smoothly shaved, as it always was, and he had the appearance of an actor. His walk then, as ever after, was peculiar. His step was short, and when he went to his seat, there was something in his movement which suggested a bird alighting in a hesitating way from a flight. His quick and all-comprehending glance, and that peculiar jerking of the head, bore out the comparison in other respects." Macdonald's strength lay in the fact that he was a great debater, as opposed to an orator. Always quick with a rebuttal, Macdonald was especially knowledgeable in parliamentary rules and election law.

While Macdonald was in Montreal, Isabella remained in Kingston, suffering from illness, during which time she became addicted to liquid opium. Macdonald's sisters, Louisa and Margaret, took care of their beloved, ailing mother, who was recovering from another stroke. Isabella continued to suffer from many maladies over the years, always in pain and forever an invalid. The intervening years were torturous for John A. and Isabella, as her infirmities placed great strain on their marriage. Macdonald frequently visited less than reputable drinking establishments while in Montreal, hoping to ease the stress of his home life.

Although Isabella's doctor suspected that her illnesses were hysterical in nature, it was advised that Macdonald take his wife to a warmer climate in the fall of 1845. The destination decided upon was Savannah, Georgia, where Isabella's sisters lived. On the way, they had to stop in Philadelphia because his wife's health seemed to be worsening. Even while Isabella convalesced in the City of Brotherly Love, Macdonald availed himself of the finer attributes of the city during the long bouts of sleep his wife experienced. The dapper and dashing John A. made the rounds with a bevy of ladies while sojourning in Philadelphia.

By November, the couple arrived in Georgia. After six months, Macdonald returned to Canada, while Isabella remained in the United States for another three years.

He visited her in New York in 1846, only to be informed that his wife was pregnant with their son, John Alexander, who was born in August 1847.

Isabella Clark Macdonald. Artist unknown.
(Wikimedia Commons)

Despite his personal problems, Macdonald's career still managed to gain momentum. He was made a Queen's Counsel in 1846. He was also invited to accept the position of Solicitor General, but he declined. On May 9, 1847, Macdonald accepted the position of Receiver General. This appointment required even more of Macdonald's attention than anything previously endeavoured. As Isabella's due date was approaching, Macdonald's mother, Helen, suffered yet another stroke. Along with Isabella's worsening condition in New York, the often conflicting reports he received from the doctors, his mother's illness, his familial responsibilities to his sisters, and the impending failure of his law practice, Macdonald's finances needed a quick infusion of funds.

Macdonald managed to secure re-election in January 1848, while most of his conservative counterparts were defeated. Divisions between the moderates and the Family Compact within the Conservative Party had caused the major strife within the caucus.

Conservative leader William Draper resigned in 1847. The

country was in recession, and finally, with the electoral decimation, the entire Conservative Party resigned in March of 1848. There was nothing left for Macdonald to do but return home to Kingston.

Isabella returned home from the United States in June. Ever suffering with illnesses, John Alexander had been dutifully cared for by Macdonald's sisters since his birth. The strain and stress of Isabella's continued illnesses had placed a great deal of stress on the entire Macdonald family. On August 2, the entire Macdonald clan celebrated John Alexander's first birthday. Within seven weeks, the young boy was dead. On September 21, 1848, John Alexander Macdonald passed away from what biographer Patricia Phenix suspects was a case of sudden infant death syndrome—SIDS. Many rumors made the rounds in Kingston as to the cause of death of the youngest Macdonald, but none held any more credence than Phenix's theory.

After the death of his son, Macdonald threw himself wholly upon his law career in both Kingston and Toronto. Life seemed to return to normal for the Macdonalds. By early 1849, the Legislature reconvened in Montreal, and Macdonald took up his seat as the Member for Kingston. In March 1849, the Reform Party, led by Robert Baldwin and Louis-Hipolyte LaFontaine, proposed a series of reforms, most notably the Amnesty Act, which afforded amnesty to those who participated in the Rebellions of 1837 and 1838. Another bill put forth at that time was the Rebellion Losses Bill, which proposed giving compensation to those people in Lower Canada who experienced property loss during the rebellions. This bill was deemed offensive to the more conservative-minded individuals, as well as the English-speaking citizens of Montreal. What was not widely known in Lower Canada at the time was that most Upper Canadian people who suffered losses during the rebellion were compensated when the conservatives were in power.

During the debate, William Hume Blake began a long tirade aimed at the conservatives and Allan McNab specifically. The tirade degenerated into a brawl on the floor of the Legislature. Throughout the melee, Blake continued his venomous diatribe directed toward his political opponents. Macdonald challenged Blake on the facts and was promptly scoffed at by Blake. Macdonald wrote a brief note and directed the page to deliver it to Blake. Macdonald had had enough; he challenged Blake to a duel. Macdonald left the chamber first, then Blake. As the assembled legislators and spectators filed outside to watch the combatants, it was noticed that Blake had disappeared, unwilling to engage Macdonald in the duel. Ultimately, both men were arrested, but they were released once Macdonald reneged on his challenge.

This was not the end of the dissent over the Rebellion Losses Bill, however. In late April, a group of ultra-conservative and anti-French people went on a week-long rampage in Montreal. The culmination of events resulted in the burning of the Parliament buildings on April 25, 1849.

Macdonald was not present to witness the event, and as a result, he was not associated with the miscreants who were responsible for the destruction.

On March 13, 1850, Isabella and Macdonald welcomed the birth of their son, Hugh John Macdonald. Isabella's illnesses were still prevalent, and Macdonald's drinking was as rampant as always.

Macdonald's law practice had been at the financial breaking point for some time. His associate, Andrew Campbell, had become weary of carrying the entire load while Macdonald was off attending to legislative matters. In amongst the joy and struggles,

Helen Macdonald, John A.'s mother, suffered yet another stroke. Yet, despite the numerous cerebral hemorrhages and the various other maladies exacerbated by these, Macdonald's mother was buoyed by the birth of Hugh John.

The new seat of government, since the destruction of the Parliament building in Montreal a year earlier, had become temporarily both Quebec City and Toronto. In May 1850, when the legislature reconvened in Toronto, Macdonald was nowhere to be found. By June, he had reappeared, and within a week he was called back to Kingston because of Isabella's condition worsening. Once again, Isabella recovered in short order, but the same could not be said of Macdonald's finances. The Trust and Loan Company of Upper Canada, a major client of Macdonald's, had been experiencing financial difficulties for some time. As they were one of Macdonald's largest clients, he had a vested interest in their survival. In the final months of 1850, Macdonald presented a private bill before the legislature, whereby an interest rate hike would be permitted for his client. The result was higher interest rates made investing in the company attractive to British investors.

The private bill passed easily, and by the fall, Macdonald was on his way to England to secure new investors for the Trust and Loan Company of Upper Canada. Macdonald's objective was to entice the British Government to invest in the firm. Even though such a manoeuver was a definite conflict of interest, Macdonald wasted little time in securing half a million pounds for his client and a healthy commission for himself, thus alleviating his financial pressures.

By 1852, Macdonald had risen considerably within the ranks of the Conservative Party but was not yet its leader, however much he may have wished to be. Always the pragmatist, Macdonald always positioned himself in a place where it would do him the most good. As a French-speaking Scot—a rarity, no doubt—John A. warned the English inhabitants of Lower Canada (Quebec) that it would be in their best interest not to underestimate their French counterparts. In a letter written to the *Montreal Gazette* on 1 January 1856, Macdonald stated:

"No one in his senses can suppose that this country can for a century to come be governed by a totally unfrenchified (sic) government. If a Lower Canadian British desires to conquer he must 'stoop to conquer.' He must make friends with the French, without sacrificing the status of his race or language. He must respect their nationality. Treat them as a nation and they will act as a free people generally do—generously. Call them a faction and they become factious. (The) truth is, that you British Lower Canadians can never forget that you were once supreme—that Jean Baptiste was your hewer of wood and drawer of water. You struggle, like the Protestant Irish in Ireland, like the Norman invaders in England, not for equality, but ascendancy—the difference between you and these interesting and amiable people being that you have not the honesty to admit it. You can't and you won't admit the principle that the majority must govern. The Gallicans may fairly be reckoned as two thirds against one third of all the other races who are lumped together as Anglo- Saxons—Heaven save the mark! The only remedies are immigration and copulation, and these will work wonders."

In late 1853, liberal co-leader Francis Hincks became entwined in a duplicitous financial arrangement, whereby he profited monetarily in the sale of municipal debentures for the Toronto, Simcoe, and Huron railways. Macdonald was merciless in his attacks upon Hincks and the governing Liberal Party. By mid-1854, an election was held, and the liberals were ousted from power.

However, the conservatives, with in-fighting of their own, were unable to form a majority. Their leader, Allan McNab, appointed

John A. MacDonald

Macdonald Attorney General, and his primary focus was to build a governing coalition. He was able to do it, and thus, the Liberal-Conservative Party was born. By 1856 Macdonald had successfully managed to have McNab removed as leader. Despite scathing criticism from within the Conservative Party and from outside, Macdonald had finagled the leadership of the party. It was a bloodless coup, with Macdonald exploiting others' weaknesses to attain what he felt was rightfully his. Even though Etienne-Paschal Tache was appointed premier instead of Macdonald, when McNab was ousted, there was no mistaking who the real power lay with.

John A. Macdonald, 1856.
(Library and Archives Canada, mikan 3218712)

Macdonald was a master of manipulation. Outwardly, he was jovial and gregarious; he possessed the admirable quality of never forgetting a face or a name. He was a great conciliator who managed to keep all the disparate components of his party sewn together. No matter their political leanings or their religious or sectarian proclivities, Macdonald was the gentleman that people grew to admire, trust, and love. That is not to say that he did not have his detractors. Men like George Brown, Richard Cartwright, and Edward Blake were all noted enemies of Macdonald's. However, he garnered the greatest affection through his astute use of patronage. He gave jobs, money, contracts, and appointments to those who would become beholden to him and the Conservative Party. Importantly, he also showed his fellow conservatives the finer points of patronage distribution, so they, too, could strengthen the Conservative Party.

George Brown, a noted Reform politician, was expounding on his principal of representation by population. Brown and his supporters felt that since Canada West (Ontario) had a greater population than Canada East (Quebec), the western area of Canada should have more seats. They used Macdonald's letter to *The Montreal Gazette* as an example of the conservatives' preference for French Canadians. Many a disparaging anti-French comment was uttered by Brown during the election of November 1857, to win the affections and votes of those who were British by heritage. Despite this, Macdonald was able to maintain power, yet Brown held the balance of power in the new government. This would come to a head in July 1858, when in an outstanding political manoeuvre, Macdonald eliminated one of his political adversaries in one bold stroke.

In 1856, the Legislature decided by vote to have Parliament moved permanently to Quebec City. Despising the choice, Macdonald managed to get the members to accept his idea that

Queen Victoria should decide where the new capital should be located. The members from Canada East (Quebec) disliked this proposal because they knew that the queen would need to rely on the advice of her ministers in Canada. Macdonald solicited the help of the governor general, Sir Edmund Head, in helping the queen decide, in February 1858, that Ottawa would instead be the new seat of government in Canada.

George Brown
(Wikimedia Commons)

On July 28, 1858, during debate on the queen's choice of capital city, an opposition member from Canada East proposed a motion whereby the queen would be notified that the choice of Ottawa as the capital was unacceptable. Members of Macdonald's Canada East faction broke ranks and voted against the government. Opposition leader George Brown seized upon the opportunity, and when Macdonald and his ministers stepped down the next day, he was requested by the governor general to form a government.

John A. Macdonald, 1858.
(Wikimedia Commons)

Parliamentary rules of the day required Brown and his ministers, once they agreed to form the government, to resign their seats effective immediately, thus requiring by-elections. With their parliamentary numbers low, Macdonald now acquired a majority and immediately defeated Brown and his government. Because of Macdonald's superior knowledge of parliamentary procedure and Brown's blind desire to defeat his political nemesis, Macdonald beat Brown at his own game. The governor general even went so far as warn Brown that, should he be defeated, he would have no choice but to invite Macdonald to form a government, as there had just been an election a mere seven months prior.

Brown, in defeat, requested the governor general dissolve

Parliament and call an election. Head remained true to his word and asked Macdonald to form a new government. Many at the time fully expected another round of government defeat, with Brown returning to power. As a matter of fact, Brown fully expected that. Macdonald, however, was up to the challenge. In what has been dubbed "The Double Shuffle," Macdonald legally swore in his previous cabinet ministers into new positions. Macdonald, for instance, became the new postmaster general. The next day, he switched everybody back to their original cabinet positions. To feign fairness, Head appointed George Etienne Cartier as Premier and Macdonald as Deputy. The destruction of George Brown was complete. Shortly after his final defeat, George Brown left politics and returned to work at his newspaper, *The Globe*, where he wrote diatribes attempting to besmirch Macdonald's name.

The incident served to cement Macdonald's ascendancy on the Canadian political scene. His star had now most certainly risen. Many of his compatriots in Parliament felt that he had fraudulently obtained power with his "Double Shuffle." Macdonald replied to his critics, "It is a charge that I am a dishonourable man, a charge that the representative of our sovereign, myself, and all my colleagues, if they have any concern in the matter, are alike dishonourable conspirators, and here in my place in parliament, I say it is *false as Hell*." Privately, though, Macdonald, referring to Brown and the whole affair, stated, "Some fish require to be toyed with. A prudent fish will play around with bait some time before he takes it, but in this instance, the fish scarcely waited till the bait was let down."

On December 28, 1857, Isabella Macdonald passed away, leaving her husband and seven-year-old son to mourn her. She was forty-eight when she died. Despite his sorrow, Macdonald returned to Toronto a mere six days after Isabella's death, leaving young Hugh in the care of his sister Margaret and her husband in Kingston. Driven to succeed in the political realm, not even the death of his wife made him waver from his course. Never close to his son Hugh and increasingly impervious to Isabella's infirmity, Macdonald was now free to pursue that which he most desired: political power.

CHAPTER 4
THE CONFEDERATION OF CANADA

By the late 1850s and into the early 1860s, Canada was experiencing a period of great prosperity and economic growth. Railway lines were growing at a fast rate. The country was benefitting from the Reciprocity Treaty with the United States, which gave Canadians a free trade pact with their southern neighbour.

Relations between Upper and Lower Canada were worsening. George Brown's call for representation by population was making inroads not only with those in Upper Canada but within Macdonald's Conservative Party. With nearly three hundred thousand more people than in Lower Canada, the rumblings were getting louder at both ends of Canada—those who wanted more seats and those who wished for the status quo to remain. Brown stirred the pot by suggesting the two Canadas separate. Tired of Lower Canada's influence, Brown wanted representation by population but would settle for a complete severing of the two Canadas.

Macdonald opposed this. He said he was a "sincere unionist. I nail my colours to the mast on that great principle." Ever faithful to Mother England, MacDonald could not fathom a Canada that was not united. Politically astute enough to know he needed

Cartier and the Canadian bloc on his side, Macdonald was nonetheless powerless to counter the religious acrimony that was present in the Canadas. The rhetoric was rife with vitriol between the Protestants and Roman Catholics, but it was especially virulent in Upper Canada. Ever angry about the political sway held by the Lower Canadians in Parliament and with Macdonald, *The Globe* reported, "Our French rulers are not over particular, we are sorry to say, and we are powerless. Upper Canadian sentiment matters nothing even in purely Upper Canadian matters. We are slaves.... J.A. Macdonald may allow his friend to buy an office. He may even take a thousand pounds of plunder, if he likes; so long as he please Lower Canada, he may rule over us." Combined with Brown's call for representation by population, Macdonald and the Province of Canada were indeed headed for interesting times.

In May 1861, there was yet another election. Representation by population was still a popular idea; it had even claimed the support of various members of the Conservative Party, as well as most of Macdonald's cabinet ministers. Macdonald held firm against it. Although people like D'Arcy McGee and Alexander Galt supported a federal union of the British North American colonies, Macdonald was not yet on board with the idea. He certainly wished for Canada to remain within the British sphere of influence, yet could not fathom the idea of creating a new country, separated from England.

John A. MacDonald

D'Arcy McGee
(Wikimedia Commons)

The conservatives were swept to power in Macdonald's first majority government. John A. had won his seat by defeating his one-time law student Oliver Mowat, who, despite being conservative, had joined with George Brown and his Reformers. Mowat, a proponent of representation by population, was soundly defeated by Macdonald in the Kingston riding. To sweeten the victory for Macdonald, Brown himself lost his seat in Toronto.

A far more dangerous and looming threat to Canada's existence appeared on the horizon, which superseded the political machinations of those who would separate this country. The American Civil War's first shots were fired at Fort Sumter, overlooking Charleston Harbor in South Carolina, on April 12, 1861. At odds over the issue of slavery, the northern states took exception to the 1857 Dred Scott ruling, which declared slavery to be legal. In early February 1861, southern states began seceding from the union after Abraham Lincoln's electoral victory the November before.

In Canada, the events south of the border were looked upon with trepidation. Those who sought representation by population warned that if they were not given what they desired, help would be sought from Washington to achieve their ends. William Seward, who lost the Republican nomination for President to Lincoln, was now the powerful secretary of state. He viewed the annexation of Canada as a virtual certainty. It was his desire to provoke the British into a war with the express purpose of giving the United States a reason to invade Canada.

Some within the American government were content to allow the Southern states to secede, provided they were able to claim Canada in its wake. Seward, a proponent of the "ripe fruit" doctrine, whereby British North America would easily fall into the United States' basket, began to speak of annexation more regularly and with more zeal. In February 1861, *The New York Herald* expounded on the theory that, should the South secede, Canada could easily be brought into the union, most likely without a fight. Supporters of this theory were said to be, according to *The Herald*, Salmon P. Chase, Lincoln's secretary of the treasury, Charles Sumner, Chairman of the Senate Foreign Relations Committee, Horace Greeley of *The New York Tribune*, and Joshua Giddings, future Consul General to British North America. However, Lincoln and his predecessors could not allow the dismantling of America. The British, for their part, were not eager for another foreign war, having just completed conflagrations in the Crimea (1853-1856), the Second Opium War in China (1856-1860), and the Indian Rebellion of 1857. The United States, which could potentially field an army of three million men, presented a more formidable foe than previously had been encountered. Since Britain relied on the United States for forty percent of its wheat and corn, they were not inclined to be drawn into the internal disputes of another nation. This did not stop them from considering recognizing the Confederacy, nor from building the warship *CSS Alabama* for the confederates.

During the first months of the war, the North suffered several defeats, most notably at Bull Run. Canadians, for the most part, were divided as to whom they preferred to win the war. Many in Canada were familiar with the North because of familial and work-related matters. In the Maritimes, favorable sentiment toward the North changed as the war progressed, mainly due to the looming threat of invasion, should the South be defeated. Trading with both the North and South, Maritimers enjoyed the best of both worlds. Even when the North placed a naval blockade on the South, those seeking to circumvent the Yanks did so while based in Halifax. In Upper Canada, much the same sentiment existed; trade and kinship were paramount.

The one prevailing sentiment throughout the Canadas and in the Maritimes was opposition to slavery. Abolished in the British Empire with the passage of the Slavery Abolition Act of 1833, most Canadians had come to view slavery as an archaic and barbaric practice. With the passage in the United States of the Fugitive Slave Act of 1850, it was a crime for an officer of the law not to arrest runaway slaves, which was punishable by a one thousand-dollar fine. If a citizen assisted a runaway slave, then they, too, would be liable to a fine in that same princely amount. There was a great outcry in the abolitionist North to this law, which helped fuel a large migration of slaves from the United States to Canada via the Underground Railroad. Harriet Beecher Stowe's 1852 book *Uncle Tom's Cabin* was a direct response to the Fugitive Slave Act. Written by a northern abolitionist, Stowe wanted to expose the cruel realities of slavery. Despite the many negative connotations included in the book, Stowe managed to galvanize many people against slavery across many continents. In the first year of publication, the book sold three hundred thousand copies in the United States and over one million copies in Britain. The book was also popular in Canada. Abraham Lincoln stated, when he met Harriet Beecher Stowe at the outset of the Civil War, "So this is the little lady who started this great war."

Macdonald, in the early months of the war, said little about the American Civil War. Proud of the British institutions that had hitherto kept the empire from imploding, Macdonald set about making sure that there was "No Looking to Washington," as some were inclined to do. It became apparent in Canada that sentiment was leaning away from the North, in favour of the South. However, John Brown's raid at Harper's Ferry, West Virginia, which originated from Canada and aimed to foment a slave insurrection, created an intense hatred of Canada throughout the South. As the citizens of Canada began to favour the South, the North took umbrage with the slight. Canadians had come to view Lincoln's resolve toward the abolition of slavery as less than sincere.

During the summer of 1861, the British sent twenty-five hundred additional troops to British North America to buttress their existing forces. On November 8, 1861, in the Old Bahama Channel between Cuba and the West Indies, the *USS San Jacinto*, acting unilaterally and without sanction from Washington, boarded the British mail ship *RMS Trent*. The *San Jacinto's* captain, Charles Wilkes, sent a boarding party of marines to the *Trent* and forcibly removed two confederate diplomats, James Mason and John Slidell. Although the boarding itself was legal, according to international law, the removal of the diplomats was not. Indignation flowed from both the United States and Britain. The American public called for war; the confederates hoped this would permanently damage relations between the two countries. Both governments involved in the affair hoped cooler heads would prevail.

The San Jacinto (right) stopping the Trent
(Wikimedia Commons)

Britain's ambassador to the United States, Lord Lyons, had previously warned the Foreign Office in London that Seward would provoke an incident. During an emergency cabinet meeting called by British Prime Minister Lord Palmerston and attended by Foreign Secretary Lord Russell, Palmerston believed Seward had most likely engineered the incident to "provoke" a conflict with Great Britain. By the end of November, Palmerston and his cabinet had drafted a communique to be sent to Lyons and given to Seward. Ultimately, after Queen Victoria engaged her husband,

Prince Albert, to review the document, it was decided that the language of the communique was too strongly worded and would be amended accordingly. The British Government were "... unwilling to believe that the United States government intended wantonly to put an insult upon this country and to add to their many distressing complications by forcing a question of dispute upon us, and that we are therefore glad to believe... that they would spontaneously offer such redress as alone could satisfy this country, viz: the restoration of the unfortunate passengers and a suitable apology."

In Washington, Lincoln, who was as enthusiastic about the seizure as most in the beginning, had decided that the tenets of international law should prevail. In early December, Minister of Finance in Macdonald's government, Alexander Galt, fortuitously happened to be in Washington at the time. In a meeting with Lincoln at the White House, the president assured Galt that America did not desire war with Britain and that they had no concealed intentions with regards to Canada. After being asked about the *Trent* affair directly, Lincoln told him precisely, "Oh, that'll be got along with." Despite these tepid assurances from Washington, Macdonald was wary of their assurances; the American public wielded a great amount of sway in the formulation of foreign policy.

With only forty-five hundred regular troops in Canada prior to 1861, the British were hardly able to defend British North America in the event of war with the United States. By the fall of that same year, the total increased to seven thousand regulars. Palmerston had wished to send an additional ten thousand regulars but was met with resistance from within his cabinet. However, Palmerston did prevail, and by September, an additional eleven thousand troops were sent to Canada. Efforts were made in Canada to bolster and train the Sedentary Militia, who were an "untrained and undisciplined" group and could hardly be expected to defend the realm. The British War Office began formulating war plans based on the notion that war looked inevitable. Incredibly, the British even formulated a plan to invade Maine to divert American forces from the expected main theatre of war in Upper Canada.

In December of 1861, Macdonald appointed himself Minister of Militia. This was a newly created portfolio and added to his already considerable workload as premier and attorney general. The defence of Canada was the obligation of the British government, yet the Canadians were expected to provide the mass of bodies required in turbulent times. Of course, they were also required to pay for their defence. The recent revolution south of the border had awakened many passions north of the border. As an early proponent of an independent Canada, D'Arcy McGee fully understood the magnitude of the current war in the United States. McGee said, "It is not the figures (of soldiers) which give the worst view.... It is the change which has taken place in the spirit of the people of the Northern states themselves. If we do not desire to become part and parcel of this people, we cannot overlook this, the greatest revolution of our times....

We run the risk of being swallowed up by the spirit of universal democracy that prevails in the United States."

D'Arcy McGee, a moderate Irish nationalist and journalist, wanted a new, independent Canada.

Macdonald preferred the British model. McGee, in the mid-1850s, believed in "a new Nationality," which called for the extensive development of railways, promoting immigration, and the creation of economic ties between the two Canadas and the Maritime provinces. He wanted a protective tariff placed on all imports to protect and promote domestic manufacturers. McGee also wanted to create a solely native Canadian province financially supported by the federal government. He hoped that the federal system he proposed would protect French Canada. Even during this time, he was anti-American, and because he saw the flaws in their "republican" ideals, he felt that his ideas had much to offer a new Canada.

Macdonald's vision was borne out of his anti-Americanism as well. He never warmed to the American way. He felt that the British way was the only correct way. Macdonald did not "... think there is anything in the world equal in real intellectual pleasure to meeting the public men of England. Their tone is so high, and their mode of thinking is so correct that it really elevates one." Macdonald felt that the American Constitution was "defective," as it had a decentralizing effect because it made all of the states self-determining, thereby planting the seeds of a secessionist movement. Anti-Americanism was pervasive in British North America in the nineteenth century, and its importance in Macdonald's story is paramount. He simply and rationally concluded that Canada had to remain British. All things American were truly second rate. Yet, this did not stop many Canadians from moving to the United States during this period. Despite the "Britishness" of the two Canadas, people often moved for reasons that were much more personal: family, money, and employment, to name but a few.

It was determined by early 1862 that Canada's defences were woefully lacking. A defence commission had established that an active militia of fifty thousand men should be established, and if the government were unable to meet that quota, then conscription should be enacted. The active militia were to be armed and receive twenty-eight days' paid training. The thought of such a large expenditure when the construction of the new Parliament was experiencing huge cost overruns made many in the Legislature balk. Macdonald's Lower Canadian members ultimately voted against John A.'s legislation, not only because of the financial hardship the country would have to bear because of it but also because of the conscription clause. MacDonald's Militia Act was defeated on May 20, 1862, by a margin of 61-54. He and Cartier resigned the next day. The governor general requested the Reformers, under John Sandfield Macdonald, to form the next government.

By May 1863, the government led by John Sandfield Macdonald was defeated. Another election did not settle or change the status quo. By March of 1864, Macdonald had managed to cobble together another government by the slimmest of margins; yet, within a few months, his government had also fallen. Canada's prospects for political stability were limited by the summer of 1864. Historian Richard Gwynn said, "It was clear to everybody that the constitution of the province of Canada was dead."

A month before the demise of the Macdonald-Tache government, Liberal leader George Brown managed to pass a private member's bill, which he had introduced the previous fall. Because of the political stalemate the Canadian parliament was experiencing, coupled with Brown's strong desire to retire and spend time with his wife and child, he introduced a bill designed to create a committee that would look at ways to reform the federation as it existed and pave the way for a more harmonious legislative process. On May 19, 1864, Brown's bill passed in the legislature. He set about constructing his twenty-person committee designed to find ways to create a new "federative system."

Macdonald had opposed this bill; he simply did not trust his old political nemesis's motives. Nonetheless, the committee began sitting the next day, with Macdonald as one of its members. The committee's findings were released the same day the Macdonald government was defeated: June 14, 1864. After Macdonald asked the governor general for a dissolution of Parliament but before it could be enacted, Brown approached Macdonald through two intercessors. Lord Monck, the governor general, suggested to Macdonald that he explore the possibility of forming a coalition involving all the parties in the House to create a solution to the political impasse. The next day, Brown and Macdonald discussed the terms for which a meeting could take place, where they would discuss the possibility of forming a coalition government.

John A. Macdonald
(Wikimedia Commons)

Despite the political and personal enmity between Brown and Macdonald, the two managed to join forces and create the "Great Coalition." Its raison d'être, according to Macdonald, was to create a truly Canadian federation. For Brown, representation by population was mandatory. Despite their political differences, Brown and Macdonald were able to achieve an accord that astounded most onlookers at the time. Although Brown only wanted a federation of the two Canadas, while Macdonald favoured one encompassing all of British North America, the two sides agreed that they would explore the "federative Principle" united, as opposed to divided. And with that, Macdonald rose in the house and declared that his request for a dissolution would be suspended. A coalition between he and Brown was created with the purpose of alleviating the political morass that had enveloped the political landscape in Upper Canada by 1864.

George Etienne Cartier

(Wikimedia Commons)

Macdonald knew that, to survive politically, he had to enter into a coalition government with Brown. Reduced to a mere twenty conservative members in the last election, Macdonald surmised that he then "... had the option of forming a coalition government or of handing over the administration of affairs to the Grit party for the next ten years." Although both men favoured different types of federations, Macdonald knew that his idea of a confederation of British North America stood a better chance of succeeding than Brown's. Brown's notion of a federation of the two Canadas was wrought with many difficulties. First, Lower Canada would be dominated by the French once the two Canadas were in place. This was made possible by the alliance created between Brown and George Etienne Cartier, leader of the Lower Canadian Conservative faction within Macdonald's party. Despite Brown's anti-French proclamations throughout the years, Cartier was astute enough of a politician to know that if he allied with Brown, he could negate the one thing he disliked more than anything else: representation by population. However, French domination of the political machinery remained a possibility, which created the renewed threat of secessionist feelings amongst English-speaking Lower Canadians, to which the British certainly would not have allowed.

Brown's machinations with Cartier would not amount to much. Macdonald, on the other hand, brilliantly seized the day by creating a vision for a united British North America that would span from the Atlantic coast to the Pacific coast. Despite his grand vision, Brown's idea of a federation held nominal changes to the current system. Macdonald's bold visualization of Canada was entirely radical—to create a pan-Canadian federation. He declared, when the Great Coalition was announced, that the federation of British North America was the first goal, and if it could not be achieved, then the creation of the United Province of Canada would be attempted.

The Great Coalition government was comprised of and dominated by John A. Macdonald, George Etienne Cartier, D'Arcy McGee, Alexander Galt, and Alexander Campbell, as well as Reformers George Brown, Oliver Mowat, and William McDougall. Under the leadership of Macdonald, the cabinet immediately began discussing the framework of the new federation. They quickly constructed the basis of the British North America Act, which would serve as Canada's constitution until 1982, when full and final independence from Great Britain was achieved.

On June 30, 1864, Governor General Monck sent requests to the governors of New Brunswick, Nova Scotia, and Prince Edward Island, asking for a delegation from the Canadas to attend their upcoming Maritime Union Conference. The governors were told that the Canadians wished to make a presentation regarding a proposal for the creation of a federation of British North America. Up to that point, there was more enthusiasm about Maritime union in Whitehall than in the three Maritime colonies. As a matter of fact, the three provinces had yet to appoint delegates, choose a venue, or even set a date for the conference, the main goal of which was to unite the three legislatures into one legislative body for a united Maritime province. After some direction from the British Colonial Office, it was decided that the conference would take place on September 1, 1864, in Charlottetown, Prince Edward Island.

Charles Stanley Monck, 4th Viscount Monck GCMG PC (October 10, 1819 –November 29, 1894), was an Irish politician who served as the last governor-general of the Province of Canada and the first governor general of Canada after Canadian Confederation.

(Wikimedia Commons)

During the preceding years, Macdonald was drinking heavily, even for him. John A. had been struggling with his health and from loneliness since the death of his wife, Isabella. Always a jovial, charming, and convivial man, Macdonald was totally uninhibited when it came to public intoxication. Once, while campaigning for office, Macdonald vomited all over the platforms while listening to his liberal opponent give a speech.

Without missing a beat, when it was his turn to speak, he approached the podium and stated, "Mr. Chairman and gentlemen, I don't know how it is, but every time I hear Mr. Jones speak it turns my stomach." Uproarious laughter ensued. Another time, while deep in the throes of depression, during a period of self-imposed exile to his bed, the governor general sent an aide to summon a drunken Macdonald back to Parliament because of his repeated and continuing absences from the House. When informed of the governor general's demand, MacDonald told the aide that if he was "...here in your official capacity, you can go back to Sir Edmund Head (the governor general), give him my compliments, and tell him to go to hell. If you are here simply as a private individual, you can go yourself!" During another occurrence, when fellow compatriot Darcy McGee was widely chastised for his disproportionate amount of drinking, McGee was visited by Macdonald, who said, "McGee, no cabinet can stand two drunkards in it, and *you* have to stop."

Increasingly, Macdonald became more and more uninhibited regarding his bouts of public intoxication. He was unabashed as to where or when he got inebriated. During one public event, when a man called Macdonald a drunk, Macdonald simply told the man, "Yes, but the people would prefer Macdonald drunk to George Brown sober." Even during the drafting of the constitution in the summer of 1864, John A. was said to have constantly shown up for meetings three hours late and drunk.

Despite this, Macdonald was a functioning drunkard. On August 29, 1864, the Canadian delegates boarded the government-owned *Queen Victoria* and headed for the Charlottetown Conference.

The *Queen Victoria* anchored in Charlottetown Harbour on September 1, 1864. The next morning, due to some confusion regarding the disembarkation process, the delegates arrived on shore in Charlottetown. At the same time as the conference in Charlottetown, the people of Prince Edward Island were experiencing the first circus to visit in more than twenty years. The excitement of the *Heather Belle* circus caused such an uproar that even most of the Prince Edward Island government was attending the festivities. As each delegation arrived, they were met solely by the provincial secretary, William Pope. Without even a cart to transport the delegates' suitcases to the various hotels, Pope singlehandedly managed to welcome all the delegates to Prince Edward Island. Because the *Queen Victoria* had anchored in the harbour, Pope had to borrow an oyster boat and row out to the ship by himself and bring Macdonald and the others back to shore. And if that were not enough, Pope was led to understand by the governor general that only four delegates from Canada would be attending, thus creating a lack of available hotel rooms. Because the *Heather Belle* circus had created such excitement amongst the province's residents, virtually all of the island's hotel rooms were booked. The ever-resourceful Pope managed to get rooms for some of the delegates while Macdonald and the rest of the Canadians stayed aboard the *Queen Victoria*.

Delegates of the Charlottetown Conference on the steps of Government House. September 1864

(Wikimedia Commons)

As soon as the conference began, the Maritimers decided to allow Macdonald and the rest of the Canadians to present their case first. The delegates from the three Atlantic provinces had handed the Canadian delegation their golden opportunity. Maritime Union had tepid support at the best of times, and the arrival of the Canadian delegation allowed them to delay those talks for the foreseeable future. It proved to be a monumental gesture, with tremendous results.

On Friday, September 2, 1864, George Etienne Cartier began the Canadian presentation at the Charlottetown Conference. He made the case for federal union, and during the remainder of the session, the Canadians listened to and answered the Maritimers' questions. The next session belonged to Macdonald. Ever the showman, Macdonald spoke for the entire session eloquently and passionately about the vast benefits of a federal union, as well as the various models of federalism available. He spoke of the pros and cons of federalism, but he truly knew how to push his agenda along in the right direction when needed. That evening, Macdonald and the rest of the Canadians hosted a lavish banquet aboard the *Queen Victoria*. Afterwards, they treated all to large amounts of liquor and champagne, the latter of which was brought with the Canadians when they departed for the conference.

On Monday, Brown and Galt extolled at great length about the financial and economic virtues of federalism. The next day, the Maritime delegates decided to move the remainder of the conference to Halifax. On the day before they left for the Nova Scotian capital, the Maritimers had one meeting regarding their own proposed union. Prince Edward Island, never really warm to the idea of Maritime Union, decided that they would only consider such a move if Charlottetown was the capital of the new unified province. A totally unacceptable idea to New Brunswick and Nova

Scotia, this would be the death knell for Maritime Union. Macdonald and his cohorts were persuasive in their arguments for a British North American federation. They headed to Halifax aboard the *Queen Victoria*—the "Confederate Cruiser," as Prince Edward Islanders jokingly referred to her—to finish the deal.

The Maritimers assembled first in Halifax in a last-ditch effort to salvage Maritime union. After a brief meeting, where it became evident that the union was dead, the Maritimers invited the Canadians back to the meetings. By early afternoon, all the delegates assembled in Halifax agreed that another conference would convene on October 10 in Quebec City to discuss a union of British North America. It would be at Quebec, where the delegates would attempt to create a constitution for the proposed confederation from the rough drafts created in Charlottetown.

At a banquet on the evening of September 12, 1864, in the honour of Nova Scotian Premier Charles Tupper, who would become a great ally of Macdonald's, a toast was proposed to the "Colonial Union." In response, Macdonald stated that he approached a federation of the British North American provinces "with the deepest emotion." He felt that the issue of "Colonial Union" was of such great importance "that it dwarfs every other question on this portion of the continent. It absorbs every idea as far as I am concerned." He highlighted the fact that he had toiled and dragged himself "for twenty long years... through the dreary waste of Colonial politics." And in a personal note, he stated that he felt that "there was no end, nothing worthy of ambition, but now I see something which is well worthy of all I have suffered in the cause of my little country." Always the pragmatist, Macdonald told the delegates that "the union of the provinces is for the advantage of all, and that the only question that remains to be settled is whether that union can be arranged with a due regard to sectional and local interests."

John A. MacDonald

Charles Tupper
(Wikimedia Commons)

And in his typical eloquence and hyperbole, Macdonald stated —with reference to the United States, shared heritage with Great Britain, and the inherent problems that this type of relationship brought—that:

"We had only the mere sentiment of a common allegiance, and we were liable, in case England and the United States were pleased to differ, to be cut off, one by one, not having any common means of defence. I believe we shall have at length an organization that will enable us to be a nation and protect ourselves as we should.

Look at the gallant defence that is being made by the Southern Republic—at this moment they have not much more than four millions of men—not much exceeding our own numbers—yet what a brave fight they have made, notwithstanding the stern bravery of the New Englander, or the fierce *elan* of the Irishman."

Macdonald felt that the "new" Canada must have only "one

common organization—one political government." He went on to say:

"It has been said that the United States Government is a failure. I don't go so far. On the contrary, I consider it a marvellous exhibition of human wisdom. It was as perfect as human wisdom could make it, and under it the American States greatly prospered until very recently; but being the work of men it had its defects, and it is for us to take advantage by experience, and endeavour to see if we cannot arrive by careful study at such a plan as will avoid the mistakes of our neighbours."

Macdonald lamented the fact that each American state "was an individual sovereignty" and that when they created their "confederation," they had only given their federal government "certain specific powers, reserving to the individual states all the other rights appertaining to sovereign powers." To cement his arguments, Macdonald said:

"The dangers that have risen from this system we will avoid if we can agree upon forming a strong central government—a great central Legislature—a constitution for a Union which we will have all the rights of sovereignty except those that are given to the local governments. Then we shall have taken a great step in advance of the American Republic. If we can only obtain that object—a vigorous general government—we shall not be New Brunswickers, nor Nova Scotians, nor Canadians, but British Americans, under the sway of the British Sovereign. In discussing the question of colonial union, we must consider what is desirable and practicable; we must consult local prejudices and aspirations. It is our desire to do so. I hope that we will be enabled to work out a constitution that will have a strong central Government, able to offer a powerful resistance to any foe whatever, and at the same time will preserve for each Province its own identity—and will protect every local ambition; and if we cannot do this we shall not be able to carry out the object we have now in view."

Macdonald now spoke to what everyone already knew but may not have realized. He stated:

"In the Conference we have had, we have been united as one man—there was no difference of feeling—no sectional prejudices or selfishness exhibited by any one—we all approached the subject feeling its importance; feeling that in our hands were the destinies of a nation; and great would be our sin and shame if any different motives had intervened to prevent us carrying out the noble object of founding a great British Monarchy, in connection with the British Empire, and under the British Queen."

And finally, Macdonald closed by saying:

"Everything, gentlemen, is to be gained by Union, and everything to be lost by disunion. Everybody admits that Union must take place sometime. I say now is the time.... If we allow so favourable an opportunity to pass, it may never come again...."

The applause was thunderous and went on for quite a while. With the conference now over, preparations needed to be made quickly for the Quebec Conference in under four weeks' time. Before they could move on to Quebec City, the Canadian delegates visited Saint John and Fredericton, New Brunswick to make their pitch in the province.

Over the next four weeks, Macdonald and the rest of the delegates feverishly prepared for the upcoming Quebec Conference. After some procedural wrangling with the British colonial secretary, official invitations were extended to the delegates of the Canadas, the three Maritime Provinces, and Newfoundland. Macdonald even sent the "Confederate Cruiser" to the East coast to ferry the participants to the conference.

On October 10, 1864, the conference opened with thirty-three delegates in the temporary Parliament building; a three-storey stone building originally designed to be a post office.

Macdonald was the dominant figure and personality at the conference. Ever the great orator, debater, negotiator, and mediator, Macdonald had to bring all of those qualities to the forefront—and then some—in the two and a half weeks during which the Quebec Conference took place. In addition to this, Macdonald used his extensive social abilities to create an atmosphere of jocularity and festivity through food and lots of drink to ensure that alliances were cultivated and exercised to their fullest.

The first resolution proposed and adopted was made by Macdonald, whereby "the best interests and present and future prosperity of British North America will be promoted by a Federal Union under the Crown of Great Britain, provided such union can be effected on principles just to the several provinces." In his defence of the resolution, Macdonald reiterated much of what he had said in Halifax. He stated that the time for union was upon them, and if they failed to seize the day, then "the scheme would be abandoned in despair." He told those assembled, many of whom were hearing this for the first time, that monetarily, British North America paled in comparison to Australia; "but, if organized as a confederacy, our increased importance would soon become manifest." He felt that, because they were isolated geographically from the rest of the British Empire and had no army to speak of, Canada was "a source of embarrassment to England." He expanded on this thought by saying, "If it were not for the weakness of Canada, Great Britain might have joined France in acknowledging the Southern Confederacy. We must, therefore, become important, not only to England but in the eyes of Foreign States and especially of the United States...." MacDonald went on to say, "For the sake of securing peace to ourselves and our posterity, we must make ourselves powerful.

The great security for peace is to convince the world of our strength by being united."

The Quebec Conference. October 1864. Painting by Robert Harris, 1884.
(Wikimedia Commons)

He continued by reinforcing the notion that Canada must take heed and not allow itself to repeat the mistakes of the United States by allowing the individual states to have more power than the federal government. He felt that Canada would be in far better shape for the future with a strong federal government "than she would be as a member of a confederacy composed of five sovereign States, which would be the result if the powers of the local Governments were not defined." And to make the point even more poignantly, Macdonald closed his speech by stating:

"A strong central Government is indispensable to the success of the experiment we are trying. Under it we shall be able to work out a system, having for its basis constitutional liberty, as opposed to democratic license. With the queen as our sovereign, we should have an Upper and a Lower House. In the former, the principle of provincial equality should obtain—the Confederacy for this purpose consisting of three divisions, Upper Canada, Lower

Canada, and the Maritime Provinces. In the Lower House the basis of representation should be population, not by universal suffrage, but according to the principles of the British constitution. With respect to the mode of appointment to the Upper House, some of us are in favour of the elective principle, more are in favour of appointment by the Crown. I will keep my own mind open on that point, as if it were a new question to me altogether. At present I am in favour of appointment by the crown. While I do not admit that the elective principle has been a failure in Canada, I think that we had better return to the original principle, and, in the words of Governor Simcoe, endeavour to make ours 'an image and transcript of the British constitution.'"

The Quebec Conference was truly Macdonald's conference. Aside from Galt, who handled the financial aspects of confederation, John A. was firmly in control. He had the complete vision of how the federation of Canada should—and would—be structured. Macdonald was recognized by D'Arcy McGee as having been the author of at least fifty of the seventy-two resolutions that would form the backbone of the British North America Act. Macdonald even stated himself, "I ha[d] no help. Not one man of the Conference (except Galt on finance) had the slightest idea of constitution making." But the strain of the responsibility and workload he bore took its toll on his health. Macdonald began to imbibe even more frequently now to alleviate the stress of nation building. Governor General Monck's sister-in-law, "Feo," wrote in her diary on October 20, "John A. Macdonald is always drunk now, I am sorry to say, and when someone went to his room the other night, they found him in his night shirt, with a railway rug thrown over him, practicing Hamlet before a looking-glass."

All three Maritime provinces had misgivings about being swallowed whole within the greater mass of British North America. Prince Edward Island specifically was not fond of the idea of confederation. Unwilling to jeopardize any of its unique island qualities, Prince Edward Islanders were an insular society. Ever distrustful of the British government, especially over their recalcitrance to buying out the province's absentee landlords so that the colonial government on the Island could resell the land to local farmers, Prince Edward Island was mistrustful of any distant administration. Feeling that their needs would be ignored because of their size and population (ninety thousand), Prince Edward Island's policy of exclusiveness eventually caused the inward-looking province to reject confederation on its own merits.

Albert Smith, 1868
(Wikimedia Commons)

New Brunswick's anti-confederates, led by Albert Smith, and Nova Scotia's, led by Joseph Howe, launched vociferous attacks on the tenets of the confederation scheme throughout the three conferences and even after confederation was achieved. Smith felt that since Maritime Union was the declared intent of the Charlottetown Conference, any discussions or negotiations about a greater confederation of the Canadian provinces were unconstitutional. He also felt that New Brunswick would be unfairly taxed to pay for others' railways and canals. Like his Prince Edward Island cohorts, Smith also felt that representation by population would place New Brunswick at a disadvantage by putting it into a permanent state of subordination within the greater Canadian political context. After the Quebec Conference, it was the province's duty to have the seventy-two resolutions passed in their respective provincial legislatures. However, New Brunswick's premier, Leonard Tilley, much to Macdonald's profound chagrin, called a provincial election based upon the tenets of confederation as negotiated in Charlottetown and Quebec City. Using the public's fear of Canada to his great advantage, Smith told the New Brunswick populace that confederation was thought up by the "oily brains of Canadian politicians" and that reciprocity with the United States, along with a direct rail link to New England, would serve New Brunswickers much better than any political union with the Canadas ever could. In the provincial election of 1865, Smith trounced Tilley and took twenty-six of forty-one seats in the legislature, although he only remained in office for about one year.

John A. MacDonald

*Joseph Howe in 1871
(Wikimedia Commons)*

In Nova Scotia, the anti-confederation movement was led by Joseph Howe. His arguments against confederation were much the same as his compatriots in the other two Maritime provinces: economic suffering and a loss of independence. His expectation that tariff increases would be disastrous to the Nova Scotian economy were correct, as well as his prognostication that it would require "the wisdom of Solomon and the energy and strategy of Frederick the Great" to create a synergy between the contrasting groups that would make up the new nation of Canada. In the end, after it became apparent that Joseph Howe could not have the British North America Act repealed in London, he went to work for Nova Scotia within the framework of the "new" nation. At one point, he was Secretary of State for the Provinces within Macdonald's government.

On October 20, 1864, in the middle of the Quebec Conference, Governor General Monck received an urgent telegram from the governor of Vermont. He told his Canadian counterpart that a renegade band of twenty-five confederate soldiers had raided St. Albans, Vermont and robbed three banks, killing one citizen and escaping with over two hundred thousand dollars. The Confederate group, led by Bennett H. Young, was recruited from spies sent north by the Confederacy with the express aim of opening a second front in the Civil War. They also wanted to use Canada as a conduit through which to communicate with Britain. After the raiders fled back into Canada, Governor General Monck had them arrested by the Canadian Militia. The United States government demanded their extradition based on their assertion that the raiders were common criminals. Even the American general in charge of the Northwest region threatened to chase the bandits into Canada, should they strike again. Ever resentful of Britain's unofficial support of the Confederacy, the Americans were in an uproar again. American newspapers began their calls again for the invasion of Canada. *The Chicago Tribune* urged Lincoln to strike north and "take Canada by the throat and throttle her as a St. Bernard would a poodle pup."

Eventually, the Canadian judge in charge of the trial released the confederate raiders based on evidence that the raid was a military action and not a strictly criminal enterprise. Furious, Lincoln enacted a law four days later, whereby Canadians would henceforth be required to produce a passport in order to enter the United States. Macdonald, on his part, was not altogether unhappy with the raid; it gave his argument of security within the British North American framework added validity. However, he was extremely perturbed at the judge's ruling, allowing the miscreants to go free. Despite the grumblings of the American press and the new passport requirements, Macdonald refused to succumb to Seward's tactics. Despite Congress's decision to not renew the Reciprocity Treaty, which would affect Canada's economy in the future, Macdonald refused to go hat in hand to appease the Americans. At the instigation of Macdonald, the raiders were apprehended and tried again before a different judge. This time, they were found guilty and extradited back to the United States, along with the ninety thousand dollars that they were captured with. The St. Albans raid played perfectly into Macdonald's grand scheme.

The Quebec Conference was a success for Macdonald. Official bilingualism was never expressly discussed at Quebec City, and no proclamations were forthcoming regarding their equality within the Canadian federation, with the exception that "both the English and French languages may be employed by the general parliament... and also in the federal courts." The only reference made by Macdonald during the confederation debates was when he stated that "the use of the French language should form one of the principles upon which the confederation should be established." Coupled with the fact that Quebec would have its own legislature and government, the Lower Canadian delegates, led by Cartier, were satisfied with the accord.

Macdonald had won the day here as well.

The Quebec Resolutions, more commonly referred to as the Seventy-Two Resolutions, formed the basis of the British North America Act. The main tenet was the creation of a strong central government, and Macdonald also ensured that the federal government would retain the powers most helpful to his centrist beliefs: finance, trade and commerce, taxation, national defence, banking, and currency. Also, the federal government held veto power over provincial legislation. It was MacDonald's wish, albeit a private one, that the provinces be made ruinously weak so that they could be eventually absorbed into the federal government. Shortly after the Quebec Conference, in a letter to Matthew Crooks Cameron, a friend and fellow conservative, Macdonald wrote, "if the Confederation goes on, you, if spared the ordinary age of man, will see both Local Parliaments and Governments absorbed in the General Power. This is as plain to me as if I saw it accomplished, but of course it does not do to adopt that point of view in discussing the subject in Lower Canada."

With the Quebec Conference over, Macdonald set about solidifying support for confederation. The Maritime delegates began a tour, which started in Montreal and worked its way by rail through Ottawa, Kingston, Belleville, Cobourg, Port Hope, and Toronto. It was Macdonald's goal to introduce his eastern delegates to his Upper Canadian friends. However, feeling the strain of the past six months, Macdonald exited the train in Kingston and immediately availed himself of the pleasures of his friend Eliza Grimason's tavern. After a six-day respite, MacDonald was back and ready to tackle the next step toward a Canadian confederation.

The Legislatures of Canada and the Maritime Provinces had to pass the confederation proposal. Once those were secured, the approval of the Colonial Office in Britain was the final step in this long process. In a pre-emptive strike, Macdonald sent George Brown to London to obtain the Colonial Office's seal of approval. Brown was told by the British that they were whole-heartedly in favour of Canadian independence. It had become apparent to Brown while in Britain that the imperial government had wished to divest themselves of their North American colonies. The reason for this, Brown wrote to MacDonald, was "the fear of invasion of Canada by the United States." Unbeknownst to either Brown or Macdonald was that the British felt that "Canada is England's weakness, till the last British soldier is brought away & Canada left on her own. We cannot hold our own with the United States." Canada was too large to defend, and the Americans, who were still in the Civil War, were too powerful to defeat. Therefore, Canada, and Macdonald by extension, had the British right where the British had wanted them.

While the confederation debates caused difficulties in the Maritimes, the Canadians began debating the Quebec Resolutions in Parliament. Lasting seven weeks, the often-rancorous deliberations ended with the passage of the Seventy-Two Resolutions by a margin of ninety-one votes for and thirty-three against. Macdonald had resorted to many of his previously used and well-worn arguments in favour of confederation. Many lamented the fact that the process was closed to the common men and women of Canada and thus not representative of anyone except those who conceived and fought for the creation of Canada. By twenty-first century sensibilities they would be correct. By nineteenth century standards, within the context of the British constitutional practice, referendums were highly impractical and most likely would have led to the total demise of confederation, as nearly happened in New Brunswick, when Tilley's government was defeated in 1865. Macdonald stated that, were any type of referendum to be held on confederation, it would be "unconstitutional and anti-British." He felt the common person would never fully understand all the details pertaining to the proposed federation. He felt that, as representatives of the people, they were fully qualified and justified to speak and decide for the people exactly what was in their best interest. Macdonald said, "If we represent the people of Canada... then we are here to pass laws for the peace, welfare and good government of the country.... If we do not represent the people of Canada, we have no right to be here."

With the passage of the Seventy-two Resolutions in Parliament, Macdonald was intent on resting for a time. Soon, though, it was evident that consultation with the British over the Resolutions would require Macdonald's presence in England. In April 1865, Macdonald, Brown, Galt, and McGee sailed to England for those consultations. While there, Oxford University conveyed upon Macdonald the honorary degree of Doctor of Civil Law, an honour which he held most dear.

However much Macdonald tried to make this trip to London seem important, the main reason for going was to mollify the recalcitrant anti-confederation sentiments in New Brunswick and Nova Scotia. The British were glad to jettison their North American colonies off the public purse and as thus were willing to help change attitudes as much as possible in the Maritimes.

British Colonial Secretary Edward Cardwell told Canadian Governor General Monck to proceed with "every proper means of influence to carry into effect without delay the proposed confederation." For all intents and purposes, Britain had given their blessing for the proposed union of the North American colonies. With vague promises of a better deal for Nova Scotia and Macdonald's "gift" of campaign funds to Tilley in New Brunswick, the pro-confederation forces were making great strides in their favour.

To compound Macdonald's difficulties, on July 30, 1865, Canadian Premier Sir Etienne Tache died. Already teetering over the confederation debates, the coalition government almost pulled apart at the seams when Governor General Monck asked Macdonald to become Premier. George Brown would not be party to this. He reminded Monck that reformers outnumbered Conservatives two to one. Finally, it was agreed that Sir Narcisse-Fortunat Belleau would become the new Premier of Canada. He was more than agreeable to Macdonald, Brown, and Cartier.

Also at this time, at a conference sponsored by the Detroit Chamber of Commerce, American businessmen assembled to discuss the Reciprocity Treaty. The American consul to Montreal told those assembled that only the annexation of Canada to the United States could end this problem. Macdonald again used his familiar arguments to buttress support for confederation. But other storms were brewing.

On April 9, 1865, General Lee surrendered to Grant at the Appomattox Court House in Virginia, ending the American Civil War. Five days later, President Lincoln was assassinated, throwing a nation into mourning. Throughout the spring and early summer of 1865, because of the end of the civil war, the Northern armies demobilized at an accelerated pace. While easing the possible threat of a massive army invading Canada, some Irish American soldiers, who were able to buy their rifles back from the army, were coming together to strike at the heart of British imperialism in North America and achieve independence for their Irish homeland.

The charge of the Fenians (left) under Colonel John O'Neill at the Battle of Ridgeway, near Niagara, Canada West, on June 2, 1866.

(Library and Archives Canada C-18737)

The Fenian Brotherhood managed to get the tacit approval of the American government. While supplying no materials or men, the administration allowed the Fenians to use the United States as a springboard to launch raids into Canada. While posing a real threat to the security of Canada, militarily, the Fenians were inept. By June 2, 1866, the Fenians had launched a fifteen hundred-soldier raid at the Battle of Ridgeway. The Fenians gave Macdonald and his pro-confederation cohorts the push they needed to achieve consensus for a union of the colonies because of the military threat. Tupper managed to push the Quebec Resolutions through the Nova Scotia Legislature in April 1866 by promising to seek better terms for Nova Scotia at the London Conference and because of the looming threat of the Fenians. Tilley's re-election in May 1865 was helped greatly by the Fenian Brotherhood and a generous infusion of money from Macdonald and his friends, which would help counteract the funds supplied to the anti-confederates in the province by "sympathetic" Americans.

The stage was now set for the final act in the confederation saga. By the end of July 1866, the Maritimers were in London to complete the confederation deal. Surprisingly, Macdonald and the other Canadians had not yet arrived in London. The British government of Lord John Russell was defeated because of its Reform Bill, and the much weaker government of Lord Derby had assumed power. The considerable forward motion that the confederation scheme had accumulated ground to a halt. Macdonald had begun drinking heavily again, and as usual, most things got pushed to the wayside when Macdonald was on a binge.

Increasingly, Macdonald was being pressured from all quarters to go to London. Tupper needed confederation before he had to, by law, call an election within nine months. Governor General Monck threatened to resign if Macdonald did not pick up the pace and get a deal done. Macdonald did not pick up the pace at all. In addition to John A.'s considerable drinking, he also wanted to make sure that there would be little time between the agreement on a revised constitution by the confederation delegates and its introduction to the British Parliament. His goal was to prevent any changes to the Quebec Resolutions—changes which would cause confederation to be scrapped because a revised document would not be the same as the one passed in the various legislatures.

Many forces combined to create the favourable conditions for the London Conference. Macdonald, of course, was the main driving force. Annexation by the United States, the Fenian raids, and Britain's "turning of the screw" to the Maritimers—whereby, if they wished to remain British (which they did), they would have to be a part of Canadian confederation—all worked together to get all the parties to this pivotal point in Canadian history.

Macdonald and the rest of the Canadians finally arrived in London at the end of November, and the London Conference officially began on December 4, 1866. The first item on the agenda for the delegates was to elect Macdonald to the chairmanship of the conference. The second item was to create a news blackout on the conference. By not allowing details on the conference to emerge, Macdonald had hoped that the fuel for the anti-confederation faction would be non-existent. And his ploy worked.

Unsurprisingly, Macdonald experienced bouts of drunkenness while at the conference. On one occasion, while staying at the colonial secretary's home, Macdonald retired to bed to read a newspaper after having too much to drink. He fell asleep and awoke to find his "bed, bed clothes and curtains all on fire." After extinguishing the fire with Cartier's assistance, Macdonald realized that his "hair, forehead & hands (were) scorched." Because of these burns and a shoulder injury, MacDonald was incapacitated for the better part of ten days.

Macdonald's aim was to finish this conference as quickly as possible and limit the changes made to the Quebec Resolutions. He was also concerned about the tenuousness of Lord Derby's government. If it was defeated, then the act of having confederation passed in the British Parliament would be delayed by an election. In fact, if the delay went past May 1867, then there was a good chance Tupper and his Nova Scotian government could be defeated in their mandatory election, thus causing the whole confederation deal to unravel with devastating consequences.

The delegates managed to get through most of the details for the new federal framework in relatively good time. One of the more important issues tackled was the naming of the new country. Macdonald wanted it to be called the "Kingdom of Canada." However, the British government felt that the United States would not take kindly to such an overt reference to the monarchy and British imperialism. New Brunswick's Leonard Tilley referred to Psalm 72, which stated, "He shall have dominion also from sea to sea, and from the river unto the ends of the earth." The confederation delegates felt that the new country should be the "Dominion of Canada" and that it would extend "from sea to sea."

John A. MacDonald

Leonard Tilley, 1869

(Wikimedia Commons)

The British North America Act was passed in the British Parliament on March 8, 1867. The new country was to come into existence on July 1, 1867. Macdonald had accomplished most of what he had set out to accomplish. He had created a constitution which gave the country a centralized government with far-reaching powers, as well as all the unassigned powers. The federal government could also veto provincial legislation; however, no provision was ever made so that amendments could be made to the constitution. Little mention was made of Indigenous rights, yet minority rights were ensconced in the constitution, as well as free trade amongst the provinces. Also, it made provision for a railway eastward to Halifax and for expansion westward, eventually to the Pacific coast and north to the Arctic Ocean, thus fulfilling the mantra of "from sea to sea."

While attending the London Conference, Macdonald was able to attend to some personal business as well. A widower for the past ten years since the death of his wife, Isabella, MacDonald had struggled greatly with loneliness.

Amongst his many idiosyncrasies, depression had caused Macdonald to re-examine his personal life. Separated from his son Hugh John, who was raised by his sister Margaret and her husband, Macdonald repeatedly fell into a pattern of drunkenness when life challenged him. He always rebounded, yet the unbridled loneliness wreaked havoc on him. MacDonald first met Susan Agnes Bernard in 1856, while dining with her brother in Toronto. Macdonald was instantly taken with the then twenty-year-old Agnes. Another eleven years passed before their union took place.

Agnes Macdonald, 1868.
(Library and Archives Canada mikan 3496598)

The pair was ideally suited for each other. Both were extremely fond of power. Agnes stated, "My love of power is strong, so strong that sometimes I dread; it influences me when I imagine I am influenced by a sense of right." Macdonald stated, "I don't care for office for the sake of power; for the sake of carrying out my own views of what's best for the country." Agnes's brother Hewitt was one of Macdonald's senior civil aides, and therefore, he was privy to John A.'s alcoholic proclivities. Hewitt was not in favour of a union between his boss and his sister, as he was all too aware of Macdonald's true self. Regardless of whether Agnes felt that she could change this leopard's spots, she soon learned that such a feat was more daunting than first believed, but she mastered it nonetheless.

Macdonald had wooed many women in his lifetime, but none captivated him as Agnes had done. MacDonald felt that she had the "keen wit, quick perception, a liberal mind, and a certain unselfishness of heart," which pleased him greatly. He loved her dearly, and she loved him also. She said, "I have found something worth living for—living in—in my husband's heart and love." Even though she was at times overbearing, she was also extremely intelligent, well read, and fluently bilingual. Athletic and adventurous, Agnes provided for Macdonald the emotional stability that had eluded him for most of his life. Macdonald and Agnes were married on February 16, 1867, at St. George's Church in London.

CHAPTER 5

PRIME MINISTER OF CANADA

Confederation Day, on July 1, 1867, was a day of mixed feelings, depending on where one lived in Canada. In Ottawa, the mood was exuberant. At the stroke of midnight, a one hundred and one-gun salute welcomed the new country into existence. In most of Ontario, there was great jubilation, with parades, picnics, fireworks, and even cricket matches. In Quebec, Confederation Day was greeted solemnly and quietly, with little fanfare. In Nova Scotia, many newspapers placed a black border around their front page to mark their displeasure. Nova Scotians also displayed their dismay by putting up black drapes in their homes, as well as putting their flags at half-mast.

Overall, despite these few shows of discontent, Canadians welcomed the new nation with open arms and hearts. Macdonald was made a Knight Commander of the Bath, henceforth known as Sir John A. Macdonald. Also, on Canada Day, the governor general appointed Macdonald the nation's first prime minister. Cartier, though, had only been made a "companion" of the same order, as had Galt. Cartier felt that this was a personal insult and, worse than that, a slap in the face for Quebec. As a result, Cartier declined the honour, as did Galt, although he would become Canada's first Minister of Finance. A few months later, though, the title of Baronet would be conferred on Cartier, allowing him to be referred to as Sir George Etienne Cartier, equal to that of John A. Galt, was also honoured shortly thereafter. He was made a Knight Commander of the Order of St. Michael and St. George. But the new nation was facing many more immediate obstacles; according to Macdonald, "Confederation is only yet the gristle, and it will require five years more before it hardens into bone." Most notable of the impending problems was the recalcitrant Nova Scotia's desire to exit the union; the non-completion of the Intercolonial Railway accounted for one of the reasons for their anger. Also, because Britain was still handling Canada's foreign policy, all Macdonald could do was to follow Whitehall's lead in this area. Of primary concern in this area was Britain's continuing poor relations with the United States. Britain's sympathetic view toward the Confederates in the American South and the North's subsequent victory during the American Civil War caused much distrust and enmity between the two nations. Annexationists, both inside and outside of the American administration, expected the new Nation of Canada to whither and fall into the ever-expanding bosom of its southern neighbour. The repeal of the Reciprocity Treaty with the American government in 1866 caused tariffs to increase on all goods exported to the United States.

Another area of concern was Canada's desire to expand westward. The Americans concluded their negotiations with Russia for the purchase of Alaska on March 30, 1867, a mere three months before Confederation Day. The Americans also had interest in the Red River Valley in Manitoba, in Saskatchewan, as well as British Columbia. Macdonald's challenge was to expand the country to the Pacific Ocean, as well as northward, to the Arctic Ocean. This meant enticing those regions to join Canada, as well as having the lands owned by the Hudson's Bay Company purchased to be included in the new nation. Macdonald also had to convince Prince Edward Island and Newfoundland to join confederation if his goal of a nation "from sea to sea" were to succeed.

John A. Macdonald, 1868
(Library and Archives Canada, mikan 3218749)

To achieve this, though, Macdonald would first have to become an elected prime minister, not one simply appointed. The election of August 1867 saw Macdonald's Conservative Party garner a majority of one hundred and one seats, versus eighty for the several parties who made up the opposition. From the thirteen available cabinet positions, Macdonald had some juggling to do if he planned to have some semblance of cohesiveness within his government. New Brunswick and Nova Scotia had a combined four cabinet posts, two of which were to be chosen by Tupper and Tilley. Ontario had five, while Quebec had the final four. Three of the Ontario posts went to Reformers, as the Conservatives were not a force in that province. In Quebec, three of the four cabinet positions went to French Canadians; the fourth went to an Anglo-Quebecer.

D'Arcy McGee had expected to be that one Anglo minister from Quebec but was surprised to learn that a protestant got the post, as opposed to an Irish Catholic. The post went to Galt, and McGee finally had to be convinced by Tupper to await another post to open. In a conciliatory moment, Tupper had given up his post in favor of a Nova Scotian Irish Catholic.

Macdonald had managed to create a cabinet that was truly national in nature while encompassing as many religious, political, factional, and regional diversities as possible. The British had never done this, nor had the Americans. Macdonald wanted all to feel included in the new Dominion. He stated in the House of Commons on April 3, 1868, that "the theory of the constitution made no such requirement, the confidence of every section of the confederation should be invited and secured by the recognition of its right to Cabinet representation."

In the election of 1867, the anti-confederate forces in Nova Scotia took eighteen of the available nineteen seats in the new Parliament. As a duly elected member of the Canadian Parliament and the de facto leader of the anti-confederate forces in Nova Scotia, Joseph Howe decided to venture to England to plead Nova Scotia's case for an early exit from confederation. There were no negotiations at all on this point. Being extremely pro-British, like most of the rest of Nova Scotia, Howe soon realized his only recourse would be to sue for annexation to the United States, a thought that was abhorrent to the fiercely loyal subject of Her Majesty's empire. Tupper was aware of the dilemma Howe faced, but more importantly, Macdonald knew it and moved quickly to exploit Howe's weakness. At a "convention" held in Halifax in August 1868, Howe drew together anti-confederate politicians of all stripes to weigh their options. Sensing an opening, Macdonald quickly assembled a delegation, including his wife Agnes, who represented the softer side of Macdonald. The delegation traveled to Halifax to counteract the machinations of those who would tear Macdonald's Canada apart. Although he did not allow his group to participate in the convention, Macdonald nonetheless doused the anti-confederate fires by offering Howe a cabinet position and by sweetening the financial compensation to be given to Nova Scotia. By mid-1869, the crisis had been averted.

By 1868, Macdonald's personal financial situation was dire. Due to the financial improprieties of his previous law partner, who died in 1864, Macdonald realized that he been saddled with a sixty-four-thousand-dollar debt (one million dollars in today's funds). The Commercial Bank of Canada, Macdonald's primary creditor, had become insolvent. Although Galt tried to solicit Macdonald's assistance in the cabinet to save the bank, Macdonald refused, and the bank ceased to exist. As a result, Macdonald's debt was sold to Hugh Allan, one of Canada's wealthiest men; in April 1869, Allan called in that debt. Despite repeated attempts to sell various properties, Macdonald was only able to raise about twelve thousand dollars. Agnes's brother had a prenuptial agreement put in place when his sister married Macdonald. Because he knew of his boss's poor money habits, a sizable amount of Macdonald's assets were subsequently transferred to Agnes upon their marriage in the likelihood of an event such as this. Macdonald managed to convince Allan that, if he were to be taken to court over his debts, the likelihood of him ever repaying the debts would be severely diminished. A year later, a wealthy friend petitioned a plethora of rich personages in Ontario and managed to cobble together nearly seventy thousand dollars for Macdonald's use—with restrictions, of course.

During this period of financial instability, Macdonald began to drink heavily again. Amid his continuing money problems, another tragedy befell Macdonald. His good friend, D'Arcy McGee, with whom he had fought many political battles with, was assassinated on the steps of his boarding house on Sparks Street in Ottawa, after a long night in the House of Commons and an even longer night of drinking with Macdonald. On the evening of April 6, 1868, Patrick Whelan, a Fenian sympathizer, placed a gun to McGee's head and pulled the trigger. He was subsequently caught, convicted, and hanged for the murder, in Canada's last public execution. On the evening of McGee's death, Agnes was awake, awaiting the arrival of her husband. That evening, she experienced some intuitive uneasiness. She began to fret for her husband, stating, "a sort of dread came upon me, as I looked out into the cold, still bright moonlight, that something might happen to him at that hour coming home alone." Macdonald arrived shortly thereafter, and soon after that, news reached him of McGee's death.

Only known photograph of Patrick Whelan
(Wikimedia Commons)

Ever critical of fellow Irish Catholics with Fenian Brotherhood proclivities, McGee was unyielding in his criticism of their violent ways. Macdonald had warned him of such vocal outbursts. In the month prior to his death, McGee had stated, "There is no danger of my being converted into a political martyr. If ever I were murdered, it would be by some wretch who would shoot me from behind." Prophetic indeed.

Macdonald was devastated by the news. He not only attended the trial, but he sat beside the judge the whole time. As well as professing complete and utter innocence of the charge, Whelan was defended by a Protestant and prosecuted by a Catholic. In nineteenth-century Canada, this was odd, to say the least. As a tribute to his friend, Macdonald rose in the House of Commons the night after his assassination and eulogized his friend. He said, "His hand was open to everyone. His heart was made for friends. And his enmities were written in water. He was too good, too generous to be rich. Yet he has left us a sacred legacy." Later, it was agreed by Parliamentarians that McGee's family would receive a government pension. McGee was the first and only Canadian politician to ever be assassinated while in office.

By the end of Patrick Whelan's trial, Agnes Macdonald learned she was pregnant. On February 8, 1869, Agnes gave birth to a daughter, Mary. Life for Macdonald and his wife could not be better. A new addition joined their family, their debt problem would soon alleviate, the Nova Scotia problem had been solved, and the economic doldrums the country had experienced were lifting.

However, heartache soon reared its ugly head for the Macdonald household. Within three months, Mary was diagnosed with hydrocephalus, a condition whereby water collects on the brain. Mary had an abnormally large head, her legs had not developed, and she had a curvature of her spine. With a life expectancy of ten years, Agnes became despondent over her daughter's prognosis (although Mary would live until 1933, and she passed away at the age of sixty- four). However much his daughter's condition may have affected him, John A. never outwardly complained or bemoaned the situation. He was attentive to Mary, and he and Agnes went to great lengths to make their daughter as happy and prosperous as possible. Institutionalization was never an option for the Macdonald's, yet the ordeal had a profound effect on Agnes. Denied "true" motherhood and family life, Agnes became stern, severe, and authoritative. Macdonald, as always, carried on stoically and with a single-minded purpose: the solidification of the Canadian nation.

Mary Macdonald, daughter of John and Agnes Macdonald.
(Library and Archives Canada, mikan 3624840)

With the Nova Scotia problem settled and the Intercolonial Railway between Halifax and Montreal begun, Macdonald set his gaze westward. Expansion west was set in motion shortly after confederation was achieved. Ontario had a vested interest in Canada expanding toward the Pacific and had pushed for its inclusion into the confederation agreement. Macdonald sent George Etienne Cartier and William McDougall to London to negotiate with The Hudson's Bay Company for the purchase of their lands.

Acquisition of HBC's lands—except for fifty thousand acres around its trading posts and one-twentieth of the most fertile lands in the prairies—was completed by 1869, which extended Canada's borders to the Rocky Mountains, including what is today Manitoba, Saskatchewan, and Alberta. However, the Indigenous and Red River Colony residents of Rupert's Land were neither informed nor consulted on the pending sale and purchase of the territory by the Canadians.

The United States Congress's proposal to allow a new railway to be built from Boston to Puget Sound in the current State of Washington gave Macdonald reason for worry.

Deciding to allow Canada to eventually find its way into the American union, residents of Minnesota nonetheless were more vociferous in their desire for the annexation of western Canada. With the completion of the Central Pacific and Union Pacific in Utah, and with the proposed Northern Pacific Railway running so close to the forty-ninth parallel, Macdonald feared that the Americans were planning to eventually move the railway north into Canada at the appropriate time. In 1868, the Minnesota legislature passed a resolution stating that with the creation of the Northern Pacific Railway, the procurement of western Canada was most desirable.

In January 1869, General Ulysses S. Grant assumed the presidency of the United States. An active annexationist, Grant wanted to expand American territory northward. Approaches were made to the British Ambassador in Washington over whether Britain objected to America claiming Canada. Britain had no wish to retain British North America, as was expressed by the ambassador, and if Canada wished to join the United States, Britain would not object. Macdonald was aware of what was happening in Washington.

Disturbed by the enmity which existed between the two countries over Britain's support of the Southern states during the Civil War, specifically of the construction of confederate ships which wreaked considerable damage upon Northern merchant shipping, Macdonald patiently sat on the sidelines. There was not much else he could do. Grant told the British that the United States government would be willing to waive their demands for hundreds of millions in recompense.

They would also forego any formal apology if Britain ceded Canada to them as compensation. Grant fully expected that Canada would be annexed during his administration. The British did as well, yet not on Grant's timetable. Macdonald, for sure, had other plans.

CHAPTER 6
THE RED RIVER REBELLION

Despite the annexationists south of the border, Canada—and by extension, Macdonald—formally took possession of The Hudson's Bay Company's land on December 1, 1869. William McDougall was appointed lieutenant governor until a more permanent political structure could be devised and put into place. The purchase itself did little to abate the Americans' desire for annexation. Macdonald, for his part, wished to hurriedly encourage British Columbia into confederation, thus fulfilling Canada's Manifest Destiny of a nation "from sea to sea."

Unfortunately for the Métis and the Indigenous people of Rupert's Land, politicians to the East had paid them no heed in their negotiations with The Hudson's Bay Company and the British. On his trip westward to assume the lieutenant governorship of the new territory, William McDougall and his entourage were stopped by a blockade of Métis, who were against the forced membership in the new Canadian nation. McDougall was given a note, which read, "The National Committee of the Métis of Red River instruct Mr. McDougall not to enter the North-West Territory without special permission from this Committee." The petition was signed by John Bruce, President, and Louis Riel, Secretary. Since he travelled without a military force of any kind, all McDougall could do was retreat across the American border and await further instructions from Macdonald.

The transfer in sovereignty took place on December 1, 1869. Macdonald reminded McDougall that, up until the time of the transfer, the area was still considered a foreign country under the auspices of The Hudson's Bay Company. McDougall was instructed not to provoke the Métis or their priestly advisers. In the meantime, Macdonald had cabled the British government, requesting that the transfer date be postponed until the residents of the Red River Colony were subdued by British force. Although a trans-Atlantic cable existed at the time for quick correspondence with England, the same could not be said for communications going westward. Even going by land to the West required a detour through the United States.

The Métis were incensed that their fates rested with others so far from the Red River Colony. Despite what anyone thought of the concept of confederation, the Métis, now led by Louis Riel, wanted a negotiated entry into the union. Riel was afraid of large-scale immigration into their lands and losing their way of life. On November 2, 1869, Riel and his fellow Métis occupied Fort Garry and declared the establishment of a provisional government.

Extremely self-confident but full of racist tendencies toward the French Metis, McDougall ignored his orders to remain in Pembina, North Dakota. On December 1, he proceeded across the U.S.-Canadian border, placed a flag at an abandoned Hudson's Bay Post, and proclaimed the territory as the possession of Canada and himself Lieutenant Governor of the colony. He then instructed his senior officer, Colonel John Stoughton Dennis, to go to Red River and gather enough sympathizers together to "attack, arrest, disarm or disperse" Riel and the rest of the rebels.

John A. MacDonald

Louis Riel, 1870
(Wikimedia Commons)

The implications of this ill-conceived move were huge. Macdonald had written instructions to McDougall, outlining his opposition to the precise actions he ultimately did.

Unfortunately, for all concerned, Macdonald's missive did not make it to Pembina in time to prevent McDougall from engaging in his grievous action. If he had received Macdonald's instructions, he would have read that Macdonald wished for him not to proceed across the border until instructed because in doing so, The Hudson Bay Company's responsibility for the colony would cease immediately. Because he had no army in which to enforce Canadian law or sovereignty, MacDougall, by crossing the border and declaring an end to the HBC's rule, would only create an atmosphere of utter chaos. Macdonald said, "In such a case, no matter how the anarchy is produced, it is quite open in the law of Nations for the inhabitants to form a Government *ex necessitate* [from necessity] for the protection of life and property." Once a government was in place, they would have "certain Sovereign rights by the *jus gentium* [the law of nations], which might be very convenient for the United States but exceedingly inconvenient for you." Should MacDougall hasten across the border, Macdonald told him, it could be "an acknowledgement of such a Government by the United States."

On November 22, 1869, Riel and his cohorts met to construct a constitution for their provisional government. Riel was aided by the French priests living in the colony, who had no fatherly love for the English, as well as by a man named Enos Stutsman. Stutsman, a U.S. Treasury agent from the Dakota Territory, was on friendly terms with Riel and assisted him with the drafting of the constitution. Stutsman, born without legs, yet a capable horseman, had agitated for many years for the annexation of the Red River Colony. Despite his proclivities toward annexation, a view never really ascribed to by Riel, Stutsman appeared to, according to one historian, have ulterior motives for annexation, namely land speculation. Unfortunately for Macdonald, the educated Riel had also realized that once sovereignty was declared, the "people", as the Métis later stated, "when it has no Government is free to adopt one form of Government in preference to another."

Councillors of the Provisional Government of the Métis Nation, 1870. Front row, L-R: Robert O'Lone, Paul Proulx. Centre row, L-R: Pierre Poitras, John Bruce, Louis Riel, John O'Donoghue, François Dauphinais.

Back row, L-R: Bonnet Tromage, Pierre de Lorme, Thomas Bunn, Xavier Page, Baptiste Beauchemin, Baptiste Tournond, Joseph (Thomas?) Spence.

(Wikimedia Commons)

Because of Macdonald's choice of the inept, overly expansionistic, and racist McDougall, Canada's westward momentum could have been halted, thus allowing the Americans to fill the breach. Macdonald had misjudged much of the situation in the Red River from the outset. First was the appointment of McDougall. Second, he failed to realize that the Métis, a strong and fiercely proud and independent people, would never succumb to being subjugated without having some type of voice in their future. Next, Macdonald had little knowledge of the Northwest Territory, nor did he attempt to familiarize himself with the area or the people. Blunders of various stripes converged to create the situation Macdonald had found himself in. Sending Joseph Howe to Red River Colony was certainly one. Having negotiated better and more lucrative terms for Nova Scotia, Howe was sent to the colony on a fact-finding mission. He was not sent with any enticements with which Riel and his fellow Métis might latch onto and cease their machinations.

By mid-December, Macdonald managed to get an extension from the British Government to solve the Métis problem. On January 8, 1870, Riel became the president of the provisional government. Riel had upped the ante by demanding from Macdonald that the Red River colony become a province within Canada. During this time, the Americans were busy making plans to extend the Northern Pacific's route into Canada, while Stutsman and his various cohorts were agitating and bribing to affect a better climate for annexation within the colony. Macdonald was not dormant during this time either. He had engaged Donald Smith, a commissioner with the Hudson's Bay Company in Montreal, to go to the colony to be his special commissioner. His task was to investigate the reasons for the rebellion and to make use of the large amount of funds afforded him by the Canadian government to negotiate an end to the rebellion.

Meanwhile, Macdonald had convinced the British Government, who had first suggested it to him, to send a military force to the colony to quell the rebellion. An added benefit to sending British regulars to Red River was showing the Americans that they were not forsaking Canada to the annexationists to the South. Smith, by January 1870, extended an offer to Riel to send a delegation to Ottawa for negotiations with Macdonald. Smith met with Riel and the provisional government at Red River, and through skilful negotiations, he managed to get Riel to agree to send a delegation to Ottawa. For his part, Riel was able to meld both French Métis and English Métis into one cohesive unit and construct a bill of rights, putting forth their claims.

In early March 1870, a counter insurgency began. Eventually, Riel was able to quell it, but not before one of the conspirators was tried and executed by firing squad. Thomas Scott, a Canadian government surveyor and Protestant, was arrested in December 1869 when he and about thirty-four others attacked Upper Fort Garry. Scott was a racist who took every opportunity he had to belittle Riel and his Métis captors. After attempting to escape and for generally being a nuisance, Scott was put on trial and was subsequently found "guilty of defying the authority of the Provisional Government, fighting with guards, and slandering the name of Louis Riel." Scott was sentenced to death by firing squad.

Smith asked Riel to spare Scott's life, but he refused. Riel told Smith, "I have done three good things since I have commenced; I have spared Boulton's (one of the co-conspirators) life at your instance, I pardoned Gaddy, and now I will shoot Scott." In doing so, Riel wanted to send a clear message to Canadians that Métis demands would need to be taken seriously. While some have suggested that Scott was not guilty of any of these things and that his trial was a farce of epic proportions, Ontario Protestants were inflamed that the French Catholics of Assiniboia had murdered one of their own on "the most frivolous pretexts." Ontario demanded retribution, and because of that demand, Quebec entered the fray on Riel's behalf. On March 4, 1870, Thomas Scott was executed by firing squad before one hundred bystanders. Now Macdonald had problems on all sides.

The execution of Thomas Scott. March 4, 1870.

(Wikimedia Commons)

Because of Scott's execution, Macdonald could no longer honour his previous offer of amnesty to the rebels. However, he did meet with the delegation Riel had sent in April 1870. In May 1870, Macdonald and Riel's representatives reached an agreement on Manitoba's entry into confederation. The proposed province would be much smaller than it is today. The federal government would retain all the remaining area for their own use in the eventual construction of the Pacific Railway, while recognizing the French language and ensuring the existence of the Roman Catholic religion. Riel, the father of Manitoba, would later state, prior to his death, "I know that through the grace of God I am the founder of Manitoba."

Manitoba came into existence on July 15, 1870, but not before Macdonald relapsed and went on one of his drinking binges. During several crucial periods in April, Macdonald only showed up in the House of Commons occasionally. He managed enough fortitude to personally present the Manitoba Act in the Commons, but he had to endure withering attacks from all quarters because of his drinking, especially from his old nemesis George Brown and his newspaper *The Globe*. Macdonald was tired, stressed, and experiencing intense pain throughout his whole body. Finally, on May 6, while working in his office, Macdonald collapsed in searing pain. A contemporary observer described Macdonald's condition as follows: "The immediate cause of his sickness was the passing of a gallstone of unusual size. The agony caused by it had thrown him into convulsions. The stone would not come away, and his nervous force was exhausted by the pain. His utter prostration left the muscles relaxed, and this relaxation let the stone pass away." It was thought at the time that Macdonald was so ill that he may not survive his ordeal. Parliament went into recess, newspapers prepared his obituary, and Agnes converted his office into an infirmary. Macdonald remained convalescing in his office for another three weeks, at the end of which he and Agnes left for some much-needed respite on Prince Edward Island.

While Macdonald was recovering from his gallstone, Colonel Garnet Wolseley, a British officer and later a commander, left Ontario, bound for the Red River Colony in a military expedition approved by Macdonald. The murder of Thomas Scott had precipitated this move by the Canadian government. Riel had thought that he had been promised amnesty; all Macdonald stated was that they would consider it in the future. That day had not yet arrived. As the Wolseley Expedition closed in on the Red River Colony, Riel, realizing all was lost, removed himself and went into exile in the United States on August 24, 1870.

Major General Wolseley

(Wikimedia Commons)

With Riel now out of the way, efforts could be made to extend Canada to the Pacific coast. While Macdonald was on the mend, Cartier took the helm in the negotiations with the delegation that had arrived in Ottawa from British Columbia. Cartier had promised the British Columbians terms which were hard to refuse: Canada would assume all their debts, and they would be given six federal seats in the House of Commons based on Macdonald's grossly inflated population figures, as well as the completion of a trans-Canadian railway within ten years. Uproarious debate occurred in the Commons over the proposed cost of such a preposterous and expensive enterprise. Macdonald needed to bring British Columbia into confederation, as the Americans were beginning to knock on that door also. He had overcome that obstacle by promising cash and jobs to many of the local annexationists in the colony, but now it seemed that he would be defeated by his own Parliament.

Along with this, the prospect of building a twenty-seven-hundred-mile-long railway through the Rocky Mountains, which had yet to be surveyed, with a federal treasury of modest means was surely a gargantuan task. Macdonald, ever the wily political strategist, and survivor, instructed British Columbia's Governor General to recall the province's legislature and have them pass the confederation agreement without delay or debate. Macdonald claimed that since the British Columbian Legislature had ratified the agreement, it was to be viewed as "a treaty" because "any alteration by Canada (of the terms) would be almost equivalent to a refusal to admit the Colony into the Union." The opposition to the railway and the union with British Columbia ceased, and on July 20, 1871, British Columbia became the sixth province in The Dominion of Canada.

Now that Canada extended "from sea to sea," Macdonald turned his attention to external considerations. Britain and the United States had been informally discussing the *Alabama* question since the fall of 1869. United States Secretary of State Hamilton Fish and the British Ambassador in Washington, Sir Edward Thornton, were engaged in talks with a goal of successfully ending the last diplomatic problem of the American Civil

War. Of course, Fish had been pushing for the right to annex Canada as payment for the many ships sunk by British-built confederate raiders. While Thornton wanted to at least give the proposal its fair shake, British Prime Minister Gladstone suggested to his cabinet colleagues that "we could sweeten the *Alabama* question for the United States by bringing in Canada."

Macdonald was invited to be a member of Britain's delegation to the talks scheduled to be held in Washington in late February 1871. In an almost untenable position as a member of a high-powered delegation, with no official Canadian standing or sway, all Macdonald could do was to watch as the world's two reigning powers duke it out diplomatically. His job was, as an official British delegate, to plead for England's position, not Canada's. That did not mean, however, that Macdonald did not attempt to work for Canada anyway. There were three issues Macdonald wished to have brought to the table: Canadian compensation for the Fenian raids, free access to American markets via a replacement for the discontinued Reciprocity Treaty, and finally, the issue of American insistence that they have access to the lucrative Atlantic Canadian fishery. However, these concerns had to be included in the larger picture; neither Canada nor its interests were ever the primary concern in Washington.

The British High Commissioners to the Treaty of Washington of 1871.
Standing: L. to R.: Lord Tenterden, Sir John A. Macdonald, Mountague Bernard.
Seated: L. to R.: Sir Stafford Northcote, Earl de Grey & Ripon, Sir Edward Thornton.

(Wikimedia Commons)

Macdonald put up a fierce fight for Canada during the negotiations at the Treaty of Washington conference. At one point, the whole affair almost fell apart when Macdonald's insistence for better terms for Canada over the fishery issue became too untenable for all concerned. At the end of the Conference, Canada did not get reparations from the United States for the Fenian raids, although Macdonald did extract a promise from the British to pay for the damage done by American-backed Irish nationalists. The Americans gained access to the Canadian fishery, although it was limited to a ten-year term that included financial considerations, which would be decided by an international tribunal. (Subsequently, it was learned that Canada would receive five-point-five million dollars, an amount that angered the Americans so much that they refused to renew the deal once it had expired.)

Macdonald never got his reciprocity agreement; all he got was cash for fish. The British agreed, after arbitration, to settle the *Alabama* affair by paying fifteen million dollars, without a formal apology.

Macdonald was disgusted by the whole ordeal. He stated, "Never in the whole course of my public life have I been in so disagreeable a position and had such an unpleasant duty to perform as the one upon which I am now engaged here." At times, he even felt like he was "struggling in muddy water with sharks." Even until the end, Macdonald was trying to negotiate a better deal for Canada by threatening to withhold Canada's ratification of the treaty, which was a requirement for it to be binding on all parties. At the end of the day, though, Macdonald signed the treaty and returned to blistering condemnation in Canada over the results. The next battle for Macdonald was getting Parliament to ratify and pass the Treaty of Washington in the House of Commons.

While the press and the liberals lambasted Macdonald for selling out Canada, Macdonald was strengthening his position by manoeuvring from the British a four million-dollar loan for the Pacific railway instead of compensation for the Fenian raids. The British were far more amenable to this than the proposed compensation package for the Fenian raids, as the latter would have had a difficult time getting passed in the British Parliament. Macdonald had asked the British to announce the loan just prior to the parliamentary debate in Canada. In Parliament, John A. told his fellow parliamentarians, "We ask the people of Canada through their representatives to accept this treaty, to accept it with all its imperfections, to accept it for the sake of peace, and for the sake of the great Empire of which we form a part." Even before he left Washington, he had coerced pro-conservative newspapers to exercise a news blackout to ensure that it not feed the backlash, especially from George Brown and *The Globe*. Despite the vociferous protestations of the liberals in Parliament, the Treaty of Washington was passed in 1872. Macdonald had lost, but he had won some important concessions for Canada, and just as importantly, he had raised his own personal profile on both the national and international stage.

It was now time for Macdonald to concentrate his energy on renewing his mandate before the electorate. The election of 1872 was the most difficult one yet for Macdonald. The provincial conservatives, under John Sandfield Macdonald, were defeated in the provincial election by the Reform Party, thus making it all the more necessary for Macdonald to campaign vigorously for all of his candidates in Ontario. In Quebec, Nova Scotia, and New Brunswick, Macdonald had trusted lieutenants who could carry the load for him. However, Macdonald, who had lost some of his vigour since suffering from gallstones a year earlier, had to fight an aggressive Liberal Party who were just as adept at greasing the palms and just as well funded as the conservatives. He did all this while working on the Treaty of Washington and handling the general duties of prime minister of Canada.

Macdonald was confident heading into the election. He had faced adversity before and won, and this time would be no different. Macdonald knew that he needed more time to lay down an even stronger foundation for Canada. He stated, "I am, as you may fancy, exceedingly desirous of carrying the election again; not with any personal object, because I am weary of the whole thing, but confederation is only yet in the gristle, and it will require five more years before it hardens into bone." So, Macdonald headed into the election with the same vigour he always had, with the express purpose of giving Canada "five more years," so he could turn gristle into bone.

Macdonald decided to create a conservative newspaper to

counteract the effects of the pro-liberal newspapers, namely *The Globe*, so he could get his message across to the electorate as well.

After soliciting enough investors to start (Macdonald even put ten thousand dollars of his own money into the venture) it was time to go after Brown and the rest of the liberals. After viewing the first issue of *The Toronto Mail*, Macdonald told the editor, T.C. Patteson, that the issue was "a good one—*for a first number.*" He went on to tell Patteson, "You must assume an appearance of dignity at the outset. The sooner, however, that you put on the war paint and commence to scalp, the better."

Macdonald gave over one hundred election speeches in Ontario during the election of 1872. He participated in donating and instructed his candidates on how to dole out the endless amounts of money needed to secure victory in the coming vote. The election had become so expensive that Macdonald even solicited campaign contributions from Hugh Allan, the same man who was lobbying the government for the contract to build the Pacific Railway. He handed out patronage unabashedly and with no moral compunction. To make matters even worse, Macdonald had spent most of the campaign "upon the drink," with little or "no clear recollection of what he did." The liberals pounded him and his conservatives mercilessly over many issues of the day, chiefly the Washington Treaty and the Red River Rebellion, whereby Ontario felt Macdonald was too lenient on Riel, while Quebec was angry because they felt Macdonald was too harsh toward him.

Macdonald and the Conservative Party, in the election of 1872, managed to garner one hundred and four seats to the opposition's ninety-six. Because of the disunity of the Liberal Party, with its pro-Ontario proclivities under the stern and highly upright and utilitarian Alexander Mackenzie, many of the Maritime liberals could not always be counted on to support their party. Ontario had failed to support the conservatives as robustly as in the past, yet Macdonald did manage to garner all ten seats from Manitoba and British Columbia. The upcoming session of Parliament would be difficult, to say the least.

During the campaign, Macdonald asked for campaign contributions from Hugh Allan, the man who owned the Canadian Pacific Railway Company, one of the two competing bids to construct Canada's transcontinental railway. Allan had also funded George Cartier's failed bid for Parliament quite handsomely, albeit too late to be of any assistance, after extracting Cartier's guarantee that Allan would receive the contract to build the Pacific Railway. Cartier was increasingly ill and of poor judgement during this period; he was diagnosed with Bright's disease, a severe kidney ailment. By the conclusion of the election, Hugh Allan had contributed over three hundred and sixty thousand dollars to the Conservative Party—funds Macdonald had publicly declared would be paid back from government coffers. This created the Pacific Scandal, which ultimately caused Macdonald and the conservatives to resign in disgrace from power.

CHAPTER 7
THE PACIFIC SCANDAL

There were two competing proposals to build the Pacific Railway for Macdonald to consider. The first was from Hugh Allan, Canada's wealthiest man at that time, who owned the Canadian Pacific Railway Company. The second was from David Lewis Macpherson, who owned the Inter-Oceanic Railway Company. In prudent fashion, Macdonald attempted to have the two firms merge to create one large, well-funded conglomerate, financially able to complete the exceedingly expensive twenty-seven-hundred-mile railway line to the Pacific Ocean. Macpherson refused; he surmised, rightfully, that Allan's silent partners were American. All this happened while Macdonald was fighting for his political life in 1872.

Hugh Allan, 1871
(Wikimedia Commons)

Cartier, who was struggling politically and financially and deteriorating quickly because of the effects of the rapidly progressing Bright's disease, felt the best course of action was to approach Allan for a campaign contribution. Allan managed to sway many of the Quebec MPs, thus making Cartier his unwitting minion in his campaign to secure the railway contract. All Cartier wanted was re-election, and because of his diminished judgement, he promised Allan the contract and carte blanche to allow for the involvement of his American partners. Macdonald expressly told Cartier that he, meaning the government, would make every effort "to secure him (Allan) the position of President," but that every other matter (i.e., board of director appointment and the allocation of company stocks) would have to wait to be decided until after the election.

Allan convinced Cartier that, since the contract was his, he could reconstitute the agreement to allow his American partners if Cartier guaranteed him the contract. He did so, and in return, Allan wrote a memorandum formally stating that his group was prepared to forward the sum of one hundred and ten thousand dollars immediately for use in the 1872 election. When Cartier notified him of the agreement, Macdonald became livid. After considering whether to promise the contract in exchange for the election funding he required so desperately, all he could muster was a "No" but subsequently Macdonald told Cartier that this arrangement was unworkable and that all he could offer Allan was the presidency of the new company. Allan agreed and the money began to flow.

Macdonald's drinking had, by then, reached monumental proportions. While Cartier's judgement was impaired by a severe kidney ailment, Macdonald, too, was impaired by alcoholism. He had always delayed any important decisions until after he had finished a binge. This time, however, due to his immense fear of losing the election, Macdonald allowed his better judgement to become cloudy. He made political decisions during his continuing alcoholic stupors. The most grievous one was when he telegraphed Allan's lawyer, J.J.C. Abbott, stating, "Immediate private. I must have another ten thousand. Will be the last time calling. Do not fail me. Answer today." And he signed it! In three days' time, Abbott replied, "Draw on me for ten thousand."

All of Macdonald's monumental mistakes eventually came back to haunt him in the most unimaginable nightmare a man of his ilk could endure. In the meantime, having won the election, Macdonald re-doubled his efforts to pull Macpherson into the Canadian Pacific Railway with Allan. In September 1872, Macpherson and his company withdrew from the proposed railway project. He cited the fact that nothing had really changed; the Americans, with their own interests in the Northern Pacific

Railway, had never left the picture. Allan, of course, denied this to the government, and despite their myopia, they accepted Allan's denials. By then, Allan was beginning to have doubts about allowing his American investors to continue with the scheme, and he subsequently dumped his American partners. Things were beginning to heat up for Macdonald. In late November, 1872, he instructed his new Quebec lieutenant, Hector-Louis Langevin, to make sure he was at the next cabinet session as "there are rocks ahead of the most dangerous character." Yet, the next month, Macdonald told the editor of *The Mail*, "We have no rocks ahead for the next session."

Macdonald was paid a visit at his prime ministerial office on December 31, 1872, by George McMullen, Allan's primary American investor. Macdonald was extremely surprised to learn from McMullen that Allan had been cavorting with the American investors for a long time. He was also astonished to learn that Allan had allowed the Americans to believe they were still in the game, even though they had not been for a while. And if that were not enough, Allan had told McMullen's lobbyist in Ottawa that the Canadian Pacific Railway would merely be "subservient and tributary" to the Northern Pacific Railway. Allan told the lobbyist that one day before he told McMullen that the deal was off. McMullen then told MacDonald that his senior Quebec ministers, Cartier and Francis Hincks, were bought off with election funds in return for their support for the scheme.

Macdonald denied everything. McMullen countered by demanding that Macdonald restore the original deal or exclude Allan from becoming president of the Canadian Pacific Railway.

John A. simply told McMullen that his argument was with Allan, and only there could he expect satisfaction. Macdonald said, "If I were in your situation, I would proceed against him." Macdonald still needed Allan for his railway plan to work, so he never threw him completely under the bus. In the end, the Americans accepted a settlement of thirty-seven and a half thousand dollars from Allan as compensation for their loss, down considerably from the two hundred thousand dollars they had initially sought. McMullen also included all the incriminating documents that were shown to Macdonald, revealing Allan's duplicitousness.

Macdonald had dodged another bullet. He neither admitted it to McMullen nor tried to bribe the problem away. Yet, the problem did not go away. Speculation about various improprieties made the rounds in Ottawa, as well as in the newspapers. Allan, who had since gone to England to secure more funding for the railway, was forced into a holding pattern until the accusations ceased. Ultimately, by October 1873, Allan, because of the Pacific Scandal, was unable to secure the funding needed to proceed with the railway. He subsequently relinquished his charter. Instead of abating, the scandal became full-blown on April 2, 1873, when liberal MP Lucius Seth Huntington, from Montreal, put forth a motion demanding that a parliamentary committee be formed to investigate improprieties regarding the Canadian Pacific.

Huntington called for an inquiry because Allan had secretly colluded with American interests to finance the construction of the railway, and the government knew this fact. Also, Huntington revealed that Allan had made gigantic financial contributions to the conservatives with the express purpose of allowing them to form the next government. Unfettered by the accusations, Macdonald simply sat stone-faced during Huntington's speech. More than mere accusations would be needed to defeat the government, and in a vote in the Commons, the motion was defeated by thirty-one votes. Macdonald had survived again. Despite the victory, John A. decided to create a five-member committee to investigate the claims laid forth by Huntington, lest he be accused of having something to hide.

Macdonald's five-member committee was ineffectual, to say the least. In typical fashion, Macdonald delayed the proceedings, hoping that some miracle would extricate him from his latest troubles. It was a tactic that had worked for him wonderfully many times in the past. Macdonald's next piece of subterfuge was to create a Royal Commission to investigate the accusations, except this time, they were able to compel witnesses to submit to questioning under oath. Liberal MP Edward Blake stated that in no way could the government investigate itself, thus causing more delays, and with it, waning public attentiveness to the affair.

Just when things seemed to be calming down, along came George McMullen, who decided to release all the pertinent documents regarding the Canadian Pacific affair to *The Montreal Herald* and *The Toronto Globe*. All the private correspondence that McMullen had presented as proof to Macdonald the previous New Year's Eve was given front-page prominence in the newspapers. McMullen gave supporting documents listing Cartier's deal with Allan, the enormous amount of funds given to the conservative campaign in the last election, the names of conservatives who would receive free shares in the new Canadian Pacific Railway, and Allan's subterfuge of allowing the Americans to think they were still part of the scheme when they were not. *The Globe* asserted publicly that Macdonald had to have known what was going on; therefore, he had to have been a willing participant in the scheme.

Macdonald countered by having Allan publicly admit his guilt. Macdonald wanted to divert blame and culpability away from himself. A mere two weeks later, the same two newspapers, *The Montreal Herald* and *The Toronto Globe*, published documents that were attained through a breaking and entering at the office of Allan's solicitor, J.J. Abbott. Various telegrams purporting the Conservative Party's receipt of election funds from Allan were publicly exposed. Included was Macdonald's plea for "another ten thousand."

Macdonald subsequently set up a Royal Commission to investigate, but he stocked it with sympathetic judges who were sure not to admonish the prime minister too severely. In the meantime, information had surfaced exposing the Liberal Party for their part in the break-in at Abbott's office. It became known that the liberals had paid five thousand dollars for one of Abbott's clerks to steal the telegrams that had become so notorious in the press.

On August 3, 1873, Macdonald disappeared. It was reported in the press "that yesterday afternoon Sir John attempted to commit suicide by jumping from the wharf into the water. He was rescued, but now lies, it is asserted, in a precarious condition." *The Toronto Globe* repeated the article the next day and went on to state that "something had happened to the premier, which his friends were endeavouring to hush up." Macdonald's colleagues asserted that the liberals had concocted this ludicrous lie so that they could "feed the excitement which the publication of the McMullen correspondence, a few days before, had produced." Agnes, it was said at the time, had taken the various reports of Macdonald's death to him at the cottage in Riviere-du-Loup, to which Macdonald sent word to his colleagues that "It is an infamous falsehood. I never was better in my life."

What had truly happened is anyone's guess. Macdonald was, in fact, missing for two days. Whether he jumped off a wharf or went on a two-day drinking binge will probably never be known. He did, however, re-surface shortly after and returned to Ottawa to face the coming storm.

On July 1, 1873, Prince Edward Island at last joined confederation. Canada agreed to assume the massive debts accumulated by the railroad, as well as provide the funds to buy out the absentee landlords to extricate Prince Edward Island from leasehold tenure.

Prince Edward Island attained assurances that "continuous communication" with the mainland would be maintained year-round.

Also in 1873, another monumental event occurred, which further enhanced the nation. The creation of the North-West Mounted Police was wholly Macdonald's creation. Formulated in response to the Red River Rebellion, Macdonald felt that a paramilitary force, modeled after the Royal Irish Constabulary, was needed in the newly acquired western half of the country. Their mission was "the preservation of the peace, the prevention of crime," and their initial purpose was to counteract the burgeoning trade in alcohol from American whiskey traders. Because of increased immigration to the west the NWMP were tasked with preventing clashes between the Indigenous peoples of the west and the new migrants to the area.

In typical fashion, Macdonald procrastinated with regards to the formation of the force. Finally, it was introduced in the Commons in March of 1873. Reports reached Ottawa in August of the Cypress Hills Massacre, which occurred on June 1. Twenty-four natives were slaughtered by a group of American hunters from Montana. Initially, Macdonald allowed recruitment and training to begin in the fall, with deployment to occur the next spring. However, because of the worsening conditions in Ottawa due to the Pacific Scandal, Macdonald approved the formation and deployment of a force of one hundred and fifty men (half the original amount) to be sent west immediately.

In a deft political manoeuver, upon his return to Ottawa after his alleged suicide attempt, MacDonald managed to get Parliament prorogued until the end of October, instead of the scheduled reopening on August 13. Liberal leader Alexander Mackenzie tried to block the attempt but was unable to. Liberal leader in-waiting Edward Blake took his complaints directly to the people of

Ontario. Instead of talking about governmental corruption, Blake began talking about morals, the rights of the common man, and the decline of democratic principles. However, Governor General Lord Dufferin, in a letter to Macdonald, admonished him about the Pacific affair. After telling Macdonald that this was the hardest thing he ever had to do, and that no matter how "deeply I may sympathize with you in your difficulties into which you have been drawn in a great measure by circumstances beyond your control, I shall be bound to sacrifice my personal inclinations to what may become my duty to my Sovereign and this country." He reminded him "that although it has been distinctly proved that in numerous respects you have been the victim of the most atrocious calumnies that your personal honour is as stainless as it has ever been...." Dufferin also said that even though Macdonald had always had Canada's best interests at heart, "It is still an indisputable fact that you and some of your colleagues have been the channels through which extravagant sums of money—derived from a person with whom you were negotiating on the part of the Dominion—were distributed." And Dufferin also told Macdonald, "Your immediate and personal connection with what has occurred, cannot but fatally affect your position as minister."

It was clear that Dufferin expected Macdonald to do the honourable thing and resign. Dufferin continued, "Independent of the personal attachment I feel toward you, I have always had and still have the greatest faith and confidence in your ability, patriotism, integrity and statesmanship. I believe there is no one in the country capable of administering its affairs to greater advantage than yourself. It is to you in fact that Canada owes its existence, and your name will be preserved in history as the father and founder of the Dominion. But no considerations of this kind are sufficient, I fear, to affect the present situation, controlled, as it is, by a special and immediate necessity."

A month prior to Dufferin's letter, Macdonald had received an anonymous letter. The unnamed writer told John A. that, "Sometime before Mr. McGee was assassinated, I warned him that if he did not resign his seat, he would be killed some way. He took no notice of my warning, and you know what happened to him. Well, sir, I give you the warning. If you do not resign your seat in the Cabinet—not only yourself but your colleagues, alas, that is the whole Cabinet—you shall be the victim. You will be killed likewise in some way or other. I shall not assassinate you, as I did not assassinate McGee, but I am the cause l'auteur (believe me) you shall not see the first of January 1874. You are a traitor, and you shall perish, I tell you... Ask Mrs. McGee if her husband had not good warning. Let her show you the letter I addressed to him at the time. The country will get rid of you some way or other. It is done with you. Reflect well upon what I am telling you."

The fatal blow to Macdonald's administration was the acceptance of such a large amount of money from an individual who stood to gain so much by the conservatives' re-election. Instead of risking a non-confidence vote in Parliament, Dufferin urged him, when they met the next day on October 20, to resign and take his chance with the electorate. The next day, at a cabinet meeting, Macdonald offered to tender his resignation. As the issue was being discussed, Dufferin summoned Macdonald once more. Dufferin had received instructions from the colonial secretary that any decision regarding Macdonald's status as prime minister had to be decided by the Canadian Parliament and not the governor general. Dufferin told Macdonald that he was retracting his last letter to him, leaving John free to continue trying to save his government.

The House of Commons reconvened on October 23, and immediately, Liberal Leader Alexander Mackenzie put forth a motion of censure. It became evident quickly that the government would not have the requisite number of votes needed to survive. Throughout the next ten days, Macdonald remained virtually silent, often too drunk to stand up. Speaker after opposition speaker recounted the events and misdeeds that had brought them to that point. Finally, in a bid to save his own reputation, since it was a foregone conclusion that the government would be defeated, Macdonald rose in the House and began a marathon speech that lasted many hours.

Macdonald, looking sickly and gaunt and fatigued, told the assembled MPs that it, in fact, was Huntington who had given payment to McMullen for the papers that would ultimately doom his government. Macdonald ended by stating:

"... I have fought the battle of Confederation, the battle of Union, the battle of the Dominion of Canada. I throw myself upon this country; I throw myself upon posterity; and I believe, and I know, that notwithstanding the many failings in my life, I shall have the voice of this country, and this House, rallying round me. And, sir, if I am mistaken in that, I can confidently appeal to a higher court—to the court of my own conscience, and to the court of posterity. I leave it to this House with every confidence. I am equal to either fortune. I can see past the decision of the House, either for or against me; but whether it be for or against me, I know—and it is no vain boast for me to say so, for even my enemies will admit that I am no boaster—that there does not exist in this country a man who has given more of his time, more of his heart, more of his wealth, or more of his intellect and power, such as they may be, for the good of this Dominion of Canada."

On November 5, Macdonald and his government resigned. Liberal Leader Alexander Mackenzie was requested to form a new government. Upon his return home that day, Macdonald simply told Agnes, who had not been forewarned that her husband was going to resign, "Well, that's gone along with." When she asked for clarification, he simply stated, "It's a relief to be out of it," and retired to bed for the evening. And so, Macdonald headed into the political hinterland for the next five years, only to return stronger, politically and personally, than ever before.

In January 1874, Mackenzie called a snap election and rolled to a majority government, after Macdonald attempted to ensnare Mackenzie's liberals as he had done to Brown in 1858, giving them one hundred and thirty-eight seats to the conservatives' sixty-eight. Macdonald was surprisingly prevented from resigning as party leader by his fellow conservatives. He continued to experience withering criticism from the public and politicians over his many previous misdeeds; however, he was content to enjoy a more private life. Macdonald told his good friend, Charles Tupper, "My fighting days are over, I think." With regards to Mackenzie, he was content in the knowledge that if you "Give the Grits rope enough... they will hang themselves." With a lack of funds at his disposal, Macdonald decided to rejoin his law practice in Toronto. He was willing to remain the leader of the opposition while living and practicing law in Toronto. He was subsequently challenged for the leadership in 1875 by Alexander Galt, who received little support and later withdrew from the challenge. Galt asked Macdonald if they could return to their former friendship, to which John A. replied, "The wound may be considered as healed over, but the scar will... remain for some time." In actuality, because of the immenseness of the man and his legend, nobody else would attempt to secure the leadership of the conservatives again.

John A. MacDonald

Alexander Mackenzie
(Wikimedia Commons)

Alexander Mackenzie, Canada's new prime minister, was a stonemason and businessman from Scotland. Involved in politics since his arrival in Canada in 1842, Mackenzie became leader of the Liberal Party shortly before the Pacific Scandal erupted. There were others more capable to lead the party at the time, most notably Edward Blake, who caused divisions because of his leadership aspirations within the caucus intense enough to distract Mackenzie during his years as prime minister. Described as a dour man who was unimaginative and uninspiring, Mackenzie lacked the flair and panache of his predecessor.

Mackenzie had the misfortune of assuming the reins of government just as the world was embarking on what became known as the Long Depression. Unwilling to spend their way out of the economic malaise, Mackenzie's liberal government began retrenching fiscally, to the point where government spending almost ceased to exist. Subsequently Mackenzie also decided to slow down talk of constructing the transcontinental railway. Besides a loan, the only other way to finance the railway would be to raise taxes, and that was not really an option during a severe depression. Edward Blake was against this option, as was Mackenzie. As Blake stated, British Columbia, that "sea of mountains," that "inhospitable country," just was not worth the effort. Naturally, British Columbia reminded Mackenzie of the confederation agreement that they had signed and said that if the railway was not constructed, they would withdraw from confederation. Blake and others refused to believe the threats, stating, "They know better." Others in Mackenzie's government, however, felt that they should honour the agreement and thus created a fracture in the party that caused the railway to be delayed indefinitely.

A fervent defender of free trade, Mackenzie appointed George Brown as chief negotiator in his attempt to affect a new Reciprocity Treaty with the United States. By June 1874, an agreement was worked out between Brown and U.S. Secretary of State Hamilton Fish. Mackenzie held out great hope for increased trade with the United States; however, the Americans' protectionist tendencies reared their ugly head, and the treaty was defeated by the United States Senate. In Canada, protectionist feelings amongst manufacturers pushed Mackenzie's government to raise tariffs in areas that were of interest to them. Mackenzie, who did not want to appear overtly protectionist, wanted to use tariffs solely to raise money for government coffers. Canadian manufacturers lobbied hard for concessions but found little sympathy from the lacklustre Mackenzie. They did, however, find a voice in the ex-prime minister, Sir John A. Macdonald.

Mackenzie's government had been struggling since coming to power in 1874, in no small measure because of the Long Depression. Unemployment was rampant. Wage reductions and business bankruptcies soared, thus adding to the misery. United States companies were also dumping their excess products into Canada at rates which Canadian manufacturers could not compete with. By 1876, the liberals had done little to ease the pain felt by the Canadian public.

Mackenzie's finance minister, Richard Cartwright, delivered a budget in February of that year, which did little to ease the situation. He felt that everyone had to "atone for past extravagance and folly by the simple recipe of thrift and hard work," and that intervention would be as effective as "flies on a wheel." Along with American protectionist policies and the subsequent refusal to ratify a new Reciprocity Treaty with Canada, Mackenzie and his government's popularity plunged to record lows. Subsequently, a disgruntled and increasingly restless Canadian public began to hand Macdonald and his Conservative Party victory after victory in by-elections.

Macdonald soon seized the moment.

John A. Macdonald, 1875.
(Library and Archives Canada, mikan 3499181)

Macdonald was, because of his conservative stripes, an adherent of free trade for a great part of his political career. As Richard Gwynn wrote in his biography of Macdonald, he "always put the politically effective ahead of the theoretical." MacDonald was most certainly a pragmatist when it came to his political survival. Sensing that the tide was indeed turning on Mackenzie, Macdonald astutely latched onto protectionism to get back into power. He became well-read in the principles of "political economy," as economics was then known as, and set about to turn the tables on the hapless liberal government. Macdonald knew that even the appearance of effort toward alleviating the economic hardships was far better than doing nothing, as Mackenzie was fond of doing. Nationalism in Canada was born from the effects of the Long Depression. That, coupled with the sentiment that Canadians were "four millions of Britons who are not free," became fertile ground for Macdonald and his newly proposed National Policy.

CHAPTER 8
MACDONALD AND CANADIAN INDIGENOUS POLICY

> "An Indian once said to myself: "We are the wild animals; you cannot make an ox of a deer." You cannot make an agriculturalist of the Indian. All we can hope for is to wean them, by slow degrees, from their nomadic habits, which have almost become an instinct, and by slow degrees absorb them or settle them on the land. Meantime they must be fairly protected."
>
> — John A. Macdonald, House of Commons debates.
> May 5, 1880.

John A. Macdonald was central in the creation of Canadian Indigenous policy in the years prior to confederation, as well as the years after. He believed in the innate dominance of British culture over all others. He felt strongly, as was the prevailing thought at the time, that the Indigenous races should be assimilated into the dominant British race. They had to forego their Indigenous social structure, take up farming, and convert their communal lands into individual family holdings, with the end goal being the ultimate destruction of the reserve system. The results were catastrophic.

In 1845, a report by Governor General Charles Bagot, entitled "Report on the affairs of the Indians in Canada," referred to as the Bagot Report, became the foundational document for the federal residential school system. A chief proponent of industrial schools, as proposed in the Bagot report, was Egerton Ryerson, then Chief Superintendent of Education in Upper Canada. On May 26, 1847, Ryerson wrote to the assistant superintendent of Indian Affairs, George Vardon, stating that "the North American Indian cannot be civilized or preserved in a state of civilization (including habits of industry and sobriety) except in connection with, if not by the influence of, not only religious instruction and sentiment but of religious feelings." He vociferously recommended that Indigenous students must live "in a separate, denominational, English-only system with a focus on industrial training."

The Gradual Civilization Act of 1857 and the Gradual Enfranchisement Act of 1869 created the underpinning for this system in the period leading to and around confederation. These Acts presumed that the French and British ways of life were to be the dominant ones; thus, Indigenous peoples needed to become French or English speakers, Christians, and farmers. During this time, most Indigenous leaders opposed these Acts. The Gradual Civilization Act was introduced in the Assembly of the Canadas by the attorney general of Upper Canada, John A. Macdonald, without ever consulting any chief or Indigenous council prior to any debate on the proposal.

According to the Act, to gain full legal rights, any adult male of a First Nation had to appear before a board of examiners and show that he was educated, debt-free, and of good moral character. After a three-year trial, the adult male would then be granted fifty acres of reservation land. In other words, they would become "enfranchised," which legally stated that they would be equal to their fellow Upper Canadians, with the exact same rights and privileges. At this point, they would no longer be members of their Indigenous nation, thus becoming full members of Upper Canadian society. As well, if he was married, his wife and any children would no longer be members of their Indigenous nation. It was MacDonald's hope that educated Indigenous people would voluntarily "enfranchise," and in addition to the residential schools, that in a few generations' time, there would no longer exist Indigenous people or Indigenous reserves.

The proposed legislation set off a firestorm of protest within the First Nations. The goals of the legislation were to hasten the ending of the Indigenous land base and increase the non-Indigenous control over their lives. The government paid little attention to the protests and repeated calls for action by Indigenous leaders. This became an all too familiar response to Native issues in the decades ahead.

From the year of confederation to the date of his death in 1891, Macdonald served as prime minister of Canada, except for the four years that the Liberals ruled. Alexander Mackenzie and his Liberals continued Macdonald's Indigenous policy from 1874 to 1878. Macdonald's Conservatives negotiated the first three of the numbered treaties in Canada's West, while Mackenzie's Liberals negotiated the final four. In 1876, the Liberals created the first integrated federal Indian Act. The Act duplicated all the measures created for Indigenous populations since 1850. Enfranchisement, Indian status, regulations regarding reserve lands and band governance, and limited provisions for schooling were the main features of the Indian Act. It was these policies, as well as the time-tested tradition of treaty-making with Indigenous peoples concerning their lands, which originated with the Royal Proclamation of 1763, that "were the main elements of First Nations policy a decade after Confederation." Macdonald and Mackenzie managed to create a situation where Indigenous self-government ceased to exist, while working for their eventual enfranchisement.

In 1878, when Macdonald returned to power, he also became Minister of the Interior. Within that ministry came the position of superintendent general of Indian Affairs, better known as Minister of Indian Affairs. In 1881, Macdonald told Edgar Dewdney that, even though he was old and infirmed, "I have no intention of giving up my present Department so long as I remain in Government. Routine matters may be attended to by the permanent Heads, but Indian matters, and the land granting system, form so great a portion of the general policy of the Government that I think it necessary for the First Minister, whoever he may be, to have that in his own hands." He felt so at home and at ease in the ministry because his deputy minister was Lawrence Vankoughnet, who had joined a previous incarnation of Indian Affairs in 1861. Vankoughnet was also a family friend, as well as a capable administrator, and he carried the workload for Macdonald. Vankoughnet played a critical role in the development and execution of departmental policy until he retired in 1893.

Macdonald combined an idealized maudlinism for Indigenous people with a total dismissal of their right to keep their ancestral cultures and religions. When he advanced the idea of creating the Department of Indian Affairs in 1880, he felt that it would promote "the interests of the Indians, civilizing them and putting them in the condition of white men." He went on to say, "We must remember that they are the original owners of the soil, of which they have been dispossessed by the covetousness or ambition of our ancestors. Perhaps, if Columbus had not discovered this continent—had left them alone—they would have worked out a tolerable civilization of their own. At all events, the Indians have been great sufferers by the discovery of America, and the transfer to it of a large white population."

In January 1879, John A. Macdonald commissioned politician Nicholas Flood Davin to author a report regarding the industrial boarding-school system in America. Known as the Davin Report, the *Report on Industrial Schools for Indians and Half-Breeds* was presented to Macdonald on March 14, 1879. It made the case for a cooperative approach between the Canadian government and the church to implement the "aggressive assimilation" pursued by President of the United States, Ulysses S. Grant. Davin's report relied laboriously on evidence he gathered through meetings with government officials, representatives of the Five Civilized Tribes in Washington, D.C., and church officials in Winnipeg, Manitoba. He managed only one visit to an industrial day school, in Minnesota, before introducing his evidence.

Ultimately, Davin concluded that the only way to civilize Indigenous peoples was to begin with children in a residential setting, away from their families, so that they could be "kept constantly within the circle of civilized conditions."

Davin's conclusions were supported by Roman Catholic priest Vital-Justin Grandin, who felt that while the probability of civilizing adults was extremely slim, they had a better chance with Indigenous children. He stated in a letter to Public Works Minister Hector-Louis Langevin that the prime way to accomplish this would be to make the children "lead a life different from their parents and cause them to forget the customs, habits & language of their ancestors." In 1883, Parliament approved forty-three thousand dollars to be spent on three industrial schools. The first, the Battleford Industrial School, opened on December 1 of that year. By 1900, there were sixty-one schools functioning. During

Macdonald's tenure, attendance in the residential schools was voluntary, but after 1920, it became compulsory. Macdonald, while not entirely responsible for over one hundred years of rampant abuse due to the residential school system, did fail to foresee the abuses which would arise in the residential schools that his government created for Indigenous youth.

The Qu'Appelle Indian Industrial School in Lebret, Assiniboia, North-West Territories, 1885

(Wikimedia Commons)

These schools ended up being a disastrous failure. In 2006, the government of Canada paid one-point-nine billion dollars in compensation to surviving attendees of the schools. A blistering investigation completed in 2015 detailed the psychological and often physical abuse meted out at the schools. Recently, the terrible story was dramatized further by terrible new revelations: the discovery of two hundred and fifteen children buried near the residential schools in Kamloops, British Columbia, as well as one hundred and eighty-two unmarked graves at a residential school near Cranbrook, British Columbia. A staggering seven hundred and fifty-one unmarked graves were discovered at the Marieval Indian Residential School in Marieval, Saskatchewan, on the lands of the Cowessess First Nation.

It is not known when the children died, why, or how. Yet, the stark reality of the buried bodies has awakened public opinion across Canada to the grim realities of the residential school system. Public monuments across Canada, especially those featuring Macdonald, have been repeatedly defaced and destroyed in angry protest.

As the person who created the residential schools, Macdonald surely received his rightful blame for the terrible human death toll. However, as one op-ed writer said, "Macdonald critics slight the fact that the worst wrongs in the schools happened after Macdonald had left this earth, and could neither be aware of them, nor correct them."

By the late 1870s, the plains were amid one of the worst human disasters in Canadian history. The rapid vanishing of the bison, in large part due to American over-hunting, had deprived plains Indigenous peoples of their principal source of food, clothing, and shelter.

Throughout the plains, Indigenous people were reduced to eating grass. Around present-day Calgary, a group of white settlers reported viewing a mass of about one thousand Indigenous people so malnourished that they had trouble walking.

Macdonald was not the architect of the famine which raged throughout the prairies. He did not create the Indian Act of 1876 or the bulk of the West's treaties. They were the work of Mackenzie's Liberal administration. But MacDonald was not above taking advantage of the situation. The conservatives returned to power on the strength of their "National Policy," part of which promised to create a transcontinental railway stretching all the way to the pacific coast of British Columbia. To accomplish this, he gave himself full control over the Ministry of Indian Affairs, as well as the North-West Mounted Police.

To clear the way for the construction of the railroad and create space on the best tracts of land for white settlers, Macdonald had to ensure that the Plains Nations were fully relegated to the designated reserves. Macdonald's Indian agents purposefully withheld food to push First Nations onto reserves and out of the way of the railroad. A liberal MP at the time even called it "a policy of submission shaped by a policy of starvation." According to James Daschuk, author of *Clearing the Plains*, "Canadian officials used food, or rather denied food, as a means to ethnically cleanse a vast region from Regina to the Alberta border as the Canadian Pacific Railway took shape."

For years, Indian agents withheld food from Indigenous people until they moved to their reserves, compelling them to forego their freedom in exchange for food. Once on reserves, food already situated in ration houses was held back for so long that much of it rotted while the people it was intended for fell into a decades-long cycle of starvation, suppressed immunity, and illnesses like tuberculosis. Thousands died.

Government aid was no guarantee that hunger would end. On the contrary, in most cases, it got worse. Agents often gave only enough food to keep people alive and little else. It did not end the hunger. On some reserves, with the outdated and shabby farming equipment provided, the reserve was expected to immediately begin growing enough food to sustain itself. The policy was a complete failure, and when reserves inevitably began to again experience famine, agents once more kept rations low enough to ensure continuous hunger and discourage the presumption of "gratuitous assistance" from Ottawa. Even when food was provided, it was often spoiled due to corrupt suppliers or total mismanagement by the Ministry of Indian Affairs. In one instance mentioned in the House of Commons, "flour" given to a half-starved Cree reserve was little more than sweepings from a grist mill. In 1883, contaminated government flour killed nearly twenty people at the current location of Alberta's Kainai First Nation.

In addition to these problems, Macdonald and Vankoughnet were constantly trying to find cost efficiencies within the department, most on the backs of the Indigenous people they were meant to serve. In the House of Commons in 1882, Macdonald stated, most damningly, that "I have reason to believe that the agents as a whole ... are doing all they can, by refusing food until the Indians are on the verge of starvation, to reduce the expense...." If that were not bad enough, it was immediately followed by an even more damaging remark from the Liberal opposition benches, charging Macdonald and his conservatives of not starving Indigenous people enough. David Mills, who was Alexander Mackenzie's Minister of the Interior during the Liberal government's tenure from 1874-1878, stated, "No doubt the Indians will bear a great degree of starvation before they will work, and so long as they are certain the Government will come to their aid, they will not do much for themselves."

The miserable conditions made sure that Macdonald spent the bulk of the 1880s overseeing near-constant famines and epidemics on federally controlled reserves. In only five years, between 1880 and 1885, the population of Plains First Nations dropped from thirty-two thousand to twenty thousand. Catholic missionary Father Louis Cochin reported in the winter of 1883 that he "saw gaunt children dying of hunger... although it was thirty to forty degrees below zero, their bodies were scarcely covered with torn rags."

Federal policy had placed natives under the sway of "low and unprincipled characters," Cree writer Robert Steinhauer wrote in 1886. Indian agents had near-dictatorial powers over their Indigenous wards. With the job treated as a patronage post, a reserve could be placed under the control of an outright sadist simply because he was owed a favour by Ottawa. In a particularly heinous occurrence in 1884, Indian agent Thomas Quinn gathered the emaciated Indigenous people in front of the on-reserve ration house, before declaring them the victims of an April Fools joke and turning them away with nothing.

The North-West Rebellion of 1885 began to reveal to the rest of Canada the hardships and privations that the Plains First Nations were subjected to. Liberal MP Malcolm Cameron told the House of Commons in 1886, "In the (United States) the Indian was the prey of the frontiersman and the cattle driver; in Canada he has been the prey of the government." He went on to further state that Macdonald was "culpably negligent" in his duties to the Indigenous peoples. Macdonald's fellow conservative, Thomas Jackson, a self-proclaimed "follower of Sir John Macdonald for twenty-five years," told an angry crowd about finding starving, half-frozen Cree being rebuffed by government agents at Fort Qu'Appelle.

Jackson stated that "In the case of one Indian... within two months seven of his children died because they had not the necessaries of life." Jackson greatly disliked Macdonald's Indian Commissioner, Edgar Dewdney. "He has raised a bitter feeling that will not be eradicated for generations; he has taught the Indians to fight against the government," said Jackson.

Macdonald once said in the House of Commons, "It has been the fault of our administrations, that they have been over-indulgent. But what can we do? We cannot as Christians, and as men with hearts in our bosoms, allow the vagabond Indian to die before us. Some of these Indians—and it is a peculiarity of their nature—will hang around the stations and will actually allow themselves to die, in the hope that just before the breath leaves their body, they will receive some assistance from the public stores." On another occasion, he said: "The whole theory of supplying the Indians is that we must prevent them from starving.

In consequence of the extinction of the buffalo, and their not having yet be taken themselves to raising crops, they were suffering greatly. The officers exercise every discretion in giving them food to prevent them from starving, but at the same time every effort was made to save the public stores and induce the Indians to become self-supporting."

As the 1880s crept on, it became more and more evident that the Indigenous people of the West were suffering from extreme hunger and, at times, outright starvation. The Department of Indian Affairs continued to deny that there was a problem. "The Government is doing much to assist [the Indian]," Edgar Dewdney (another of Macdonald's friends, who was lieutenant-governor and commissioner of Indian affairs for the North-West) told Ottawa. Dewdney went on to tell his boss, "After a sharp trial, during which they will doubtless be not a little suffering, let us hope that the crisis will be overcome."

MacDonald allowed the creation of the pass system. After the North-West Rebellion, the authorities seized all horses and firearms with the express hope of avoiding further trouble from Indigenous people. The pass system was implemented to curtail the movement of treaty Indians by keeping them tied to the reserves and away from white communities. The system had the unfortunate effect of preventing access to game and disallowing prospective economic development on the reserves. Dewdney knew that the imposition of the pass system was bordering on illegal, and he told Macdonald, "To compel the Indians to live wholly on their Reserves our Treaty must be altered." The North-West Mounted Police protested the pass system but reluctantly followed their orders. One Roman Catholic priest wondered if the reserves would actually "help those poor Indians—there the agents will refuse to feed them as they have already done."

During this period, the government also outlawed powwows

and potlatches. These restrictions remained in place deep into the twentieth century.

With Macdonald's permission, large crowds of Indigenous people from around Battleford and Saskatchewan, as well as children from the Battleford Industrial School, were brought together to witness the mass hanging of eight Cree men. The eight had killed nine white men during the North-West Rebellion at a place several hundred kilometres to the east. The killing of the nine men has been referred to as the Frog Lake Massacre, but according to James Daschuk, it was nothing more than a "settling of personal scores." Interestingly, one of those killed at Frog Lake was Thomas Quinn, the "April Fools" Indian agent. Although Canada had only recently outlawed public hangings, Macdonald felt that an example needed to be made.

Once the eight Cree men were hanged, their bodies were not cut down for fifteen minutes, thus allowing the effect to sink in fully to the Indigenous people forced to watch the spectacle.

"The executions of the Indians... ought to convince the Red Man that the White Man governs," Macdonald wrote to Edgar Dewdney shortly thereafter. In fact, the North-West Rebellion fizzled out so rapidly in large part because so many Plains Cree leaders had emphatically refused to join Riel.

Among white society in the Victorian-era British Empire, it was believed to be morally righteous to supplant Indigenous nations with European civilization. In Macdonald's case his impetus was the creation of a transcontinental railway and the settling of the West all in the name of nation building. The Americans, meanwhile, forcibly grasped their country from Indigenous peoples through decades of wars and massacres. Even the Great Emancipator, Abraham Lincoln, mercilessly suppressed a Sioux uprising with a mass-hanging that still ranks as the largest in U.S. history.

One Macdonald biographer wrote in 1891, "The leading feature of Sir John's Indian policy was to keep the Indian alive during times of scarcity, and gradually wean him from his wild ways into habits of settled industry." Macdonald stated, "All we can hope to do is to wean them, by slow degrees, from their nomadic habits, which have almost become an instinct, and by slow degrees absorb them or settle them on land. Meanwhile they must be fairly protected." Macdonald failed miserably at this task. The Indigenous population was far worse off than if they had been left to their own devices. As elsewhere in the British Empire, the white men forced their will upon the Indigenous people of the conquered lands, to dire effects.

No matter who was in the prime minister's office at the time, they pursued a policy of assimilation with as much fervour against Canada's Indigenous peoples as Macdonald had. James Daschuk stated, "He had a deadline, and that's why he put the screws on so tight."

CHAPTER 9
THE NATIONAL POLICY

By the summer of 1876, Macdonald had begun using a scheme called "picnic politics" to increase his exposure and to pitch his new National Policy. Usually held on farms and organized by local conservatives, the affairs were lavish. Food and spirits were offered to people all at no charge. Macdonald then laid out his program to the amassed throngs using the slogan "Canada for Canadians" to drive the point home. He told them that Canada would implement high tariffs on goods coming in from other nations, and by protecting those industries through protective tariffs, Canada would be able to become economically independent, thus protecting it for Canadians. Macdonald also maintained that rapid completion of the transcontinental railroad was necessary so that new immigrants could populate the West and begin sending their agricultural goods back east on the completed railway. Meanwhile, manufacturers in the East could send their products west for consumption there. Also, Macdonald used patronage without shame, even when out of office. He once said, "How was it...that he without means, power or patronage...should be so received?" All Macdonald had to do sometimes was merely hint at the promise of a job or some other patronage plum. The loyalty that the "Grand Old Man" commanded was often stunning. There were many people who were devout followers and admirers of Macdonald. The inspired and unbridled loyalty which he commanded had limits, though, as sometimes he was chastised for unfulfilled promises. His contrition knew no bounds; he often listened to the rebukes and stated that he was sorry for "acts of omission and commission which I regret." On larger issues, he said, "I was acting ... for the interest of our common country." Macdonald was nearly always able to charm himself out of a situation because of his immense popularity and because people felt that he was one of them. He often pointed out, he "had worked for thirty years, and yet had not amassed wealth."

By protecting farmers and manufacturers, Macdonald knew that the West would be settled, and Canadian cities would grow rapidly as commerce at both ends of the spectrum flourished. All this was accomplished adroitly by the charismatic and extremely pragmatic Macdonald and his keen political intellect. At one of the "political picnics," Macdonald, who never allowed an occasion to besmirch his opponents slide by, stated, "It only goes to show that Providence is on our side.... While we were in power, there were splendid crops, good prices, no weevil, and no potato-bugs. We are going to have a good crop now though a Grit government is in—but the reason is this: *the Grits are going out!*" Macdonald at this time was also getting his alcohol problem under control. Lord Dufferin remarked in May 1877 that Macdonald "could drink wine at dinner without being tempted to excess, which hitherto he has never been able to do."

Finally, his body rebelled from the abuse. He told Dufferin, "My constitution has quite changed of late," meaning his body could no longer handle excessive alcohol use. As a result, he was at his political best. He exploited all of Mackenzie's weaknesses to his benefit. Protectionism had never been one of Macdonald's causes until it became politically expedient to do so, and because of its immense popularity, Macdonald felt that "Protection has done so much for me that I felt that I must do something for protection." Macdonald soundly defeated Mackenzie and his liberals in the September 1878 election, with a commanding majority that highlighted one of Canada's most remarkable political comebacks ever.

John A. Macdonald, 1878.
(Library and Archives Canada, mikan 3218751)

With a majority of eighty seats, Mackenzie could hardly contain his disgust at losing to the man all had considered finished after the Pacific Scandal. Mackenzie wrote to a fellow MP that his fellow Canadians seemed to have wanted a prime minister who "must have graduated as a horse thief or at least have distinguished himself as having chiselled a municipality or robbed a Railway Company." As Dale Thompson wrote in his biography of Mackenzie, the public "preferred MacDonald drunk to Mackenzie sober." Upon reflection, Mackenzie said, "I have nothing to regret in looking back at my course. Even had I known of the tendency of the public mind, I would not for the sake of office yield up my convictions on that (the National Policy) or on any other subject. I tried to keep Canada in line with England and in harmony with enlightened modern thought on commercial subjects, and I have failed, as better men have failed before me...." But things were not all rosy for Macdonald; he lost his own Kingston seat and was derided for being the "Do-Nothing Deserter" who went to live in Toronto after his last election defeat. His personal friend, Eliza Grimason, a local tavern owner whose establishment Macdonald frequented and his main local organizer during his many election campaigns, was absolutely heartbroken that the people of Kingston had shunned such a magnificent man. Macdonald won a seat in Victoria, British Columbia (B.C. held their polls later), but despite that victory, Eliza said Macdonald should rebuke the people of Kingston "and tell them all to go to the devil." Macdonald replied laughingly, "The country would go to the dogs if [I] did that."

Macdonald was sworn in as Canada's third prime minister on October 17, 1878. Macdonald was happy about his return to power. He remained in Toronto for a time and told a friend, "I resolved to reverse the verdict of 1874 and have done so to my heart's content." He also told an assembled group of followers, "Trade revived, crops were abundant, and bank stocks once more became buoyant, owing to the confidence of the people of Canada in the new Administration. A citizen of Toronto assured me that his Conservative cow gave three quarts of milk more a day after the election than before; while a good Conservative lady-friend solemnly affirmed that her hens laid more eggs, larger eggs, fresher eggs and more to the dozen ever since the new Administration came in." Macdonald's first order of business was to create a cabinet.

Many of the old faces had returned: Tilley, Tupper, Hector Langevin, and Alexander Campbell, thus fashioning a cabinet that was well-worn but experienced.

By that time, Macdonald was sixty-four and suffering from various ailments. He suffered from liver problems, he contracted cholera in 1879, and had not fully recovered all his previous vigour from his bout of gallstones. He was physically tired, yet he continued at a more orderly pace. His sister Louisa remarked a couple of years later, "I never saw John looking what I would call old until this time. His hair is getting quite grey." He was drinking less but did not stop altogether. In November 1878, Macdonald had to travel to Halifax to meet the new governor general, the Marquess of Lorne, and his wife, Princess Louise, who was Queen Victoria's daughter. He arranged for a special railway carriage to transport the new regal residents of Rideau Hall, but he himself rode coach, stating, "We are not going to travel to Halifax like princes but like ordinary mortals. "He and Tupper boarded the train, Tupper with his luggage and Macdonald with many bottles of brandy. And drink he did. Even as he cloistered himself in his room at the lieutenant governor's residence, he continued to drink, much to the chagrin of all who witnessed it. The lieutenant governor's daughter engaged one of Macdonald's secretaries to summon the prime minister from his drunken stupor as the guests were about to disembark from their transatlantic voyage. The secretary, upon entering Macdonald's room, found that he was "looking more dead than alive" in his horizontal position. The secretary imparted his message that the new governor general was about to arrive and that the prime minister was required at the reception.

Macdonald raised himself up halfway, pointed at his secretary with a disgusted look, and stated, "Vamoose from this ranch!"

Mi'kMaq Grand Chief Jacques-Pierre Peminuit Paul (Third from left with beard) meets Governor General of Canada, Marquess of Lorne, Red Chamber, Province House, Halifax, Nova Scotia, 1879

(Wikimedia Commons)

Macdonald's agenda for the new government was simple: fully implement the National Policy, build the Canadian Pacific Railway, and create a standing army. With regards to the standing army, Macdonald wanted to build a small permanent army of three battalions. The only way Macdonald could fulfill his nationalistic program was through funds garnered through tariffs. The tariffs that formed the backbone of the National Policy fell to Leonard Tilley, the former Premier of New Brunswick. As Macdonald's new Minister of Finance, Tilley stated, during his budget speech of 1879, "The time has arrived when we are to decide whether we will simply be hewers of wood and drawers of water." Tilley set about the task of creating a schedule of tariffs by which the government could raise funds while protecting Canada's interests within an increasingly global economy.

Tilley decided, practically, "to select for a higher rate of duty those [items] that are manufactured in the country, and to leave those that are not made... at a lower rate." The rates ranged from zero percent for goods manufactured in Canada to thirty percent on those manufactured outside the country. Items partially made elsewhere fit somewhere between those percentages. Macdonald and Tilley had to be ever mindful of offending Britain. The tariffs were to apply to all countries, as France, Germany, and the United States had done. However, it was argued that British taxes were paying for the naval fleet to patrol each coast of Canada, as well as the men who were part of Britain's standing force in Canada. Macdonald's National Policy tariffs still needed approval from the Colonial Office. Macdonald and Tilley had explored entering a Reciprocal Treaty with Great Britain but feared American reaction. Macdonald was unwilling to risk the economic wrath of their neighbour to the South. So, they had to apply the tariffs to English goods while not incurring their displeasure. Despite the intense lobbying of some British businesses, Macdonald was able to convince them that the sole purpose of the National Policy was to "promote trade with Britain." He told one British newspaper, "The chief difficulty (with exempting Britain from the tariffs) was that England had nothing to give Canada by way of reciprocity," because of Britain's staunch adherence to free trade.

Amazingly, despite increasing pressure from the British, Macdonald secured the consent of the Colonial Office, which stated, "The fiscal policy of Canada [is] a matter for decision by the Dominion legislature subject to treaty obligations."

Macdonald's timing was impeccable. The Long Depression was ending, and the National Policy was a huge success in creating wealth and jobs at exactly the time the nation required it. Most

Canadians enjoyed the added prosperity. Others, like Alexander Mackenzie, felt that "Protection is a monster when you come to look at it. It is the essence of injustice. It is the acme of human selfishness. It is one of the relics of barbarism." Challenges remained, but Macdonald's National Policy was in force. Next, Macdonald looked to the task of building the Canadian Pacific Railway and Canada's western territories.

CHAPTER 10
THE CANADIAN PACIFIC RAILWAY

Macdonald knew that the Canadian government could not build and operate the Canadian Pacific Railway. Another solution was needed. Charles Tupper, as Minister of Railways and Canals in the Macdonald government, suggested to his cabinet colleagues that the charter be given to a syndicate of prominent businessmen capable of building such a monumental railway. Tupper was approached by George Stephen, President of the Bank of Montreal. Stephen was also a noted financier and philanthropist. He and his consortium, which included his cousin Donald Smith (later Lord Strathcona and Macdonald's nemesis), had a year earlier purchased the financially challenged St. Paul and Pacific Railroad, financed primarily through a loan from the Bank of Montreal at preferential interest rates.

Within six years, they restored profitability to the railway through an extension of the line to Winnipeg. They subsequently sold it for twenty-five million dollars.

George Stephen, 1865.
(Wikimedia Commons)

By June 1881, Tupper had secured permission from the cabinet and Macdonald to begin negotiations with Stephen. Tupper believed the syndicate would build and operate the railway, as well as assume the responsibility of "the rapid settlement of the public lands." It remained to be seen how much money the conservative government would have to pay to ensure the success of the venture. By the late 1870s, the Long Depression had ended, and immigration west was in full swing. It was important for Macdonald to have a transcontinental railway built so that Canadian goods from the East could move westward easily, thus ensuring the stability and longevity of Macdonald's National Policy. Stephen, for his part, wanted as little public borrowing for his venture as possible so that his investors could maximize the return on their investment through "the growth of the country and the development of the property." Stephen knew that he would make more money off the sale of the lands adjacent to the line than he ever would from the operation of the railway.

Before negotiations proceeded, Macdonald sent Tupper to England to see if any other investors would be interested in building Canada's twenty-seven-hundred-mile transcontinental railway.

Unsurprisingly, no interested parties were found, and negotiations with Stephen proceeded. Stephen was aware that, to develop and sell land, they had to build the railway quickly. To achieve that, Stephen insisted that the Canadian government grant them a monopoly over all railways in the West for a specific period. Macdonald was not keen on the idea, but Stephen bluntly told him that if he did not receive a monopoly, he would simply bow out of the process and not build the railroad. Stephen had Macdonald over a barrel. On October 21, 1880, an agreement was constructed and signed. Immediately, cries from all quarters began, as the terms of the contract were most generous to the Canadian Pacific Railway consortium. They were to receive twenty-five million dollars and twenty-five million acres of land. They were to pay no tax on the land for twenty years, as well as no tax on any buildings (like stations) they constructed on the line for all time. Astoundingly, they were given the seven hundred or so miles that were built by the Mackenzie government; two sections were built, at the beginning in Ontario and at the other end in British Columbia. Also, they were exempted from paying tariffs on any imported materials essential to the railroad. The Mackenzie government had surveyed the complete line from Ontario to British Columbia. These two items alone were valued in excess of thirty-eight million dollars. Stephen also secured his twenty-year monopoly on all railways heading south to the United States in the West.

In return, Macdonald forced upon Stephen his demand that the entire two thousand miles of remaining track be constructed solely on Canadian soil. Stephen did not like this condition, as it would have been much cheaper and easier to divert through the United States, yet Macdonald held true to his vision that the transcontinental railway be a truly Canadian one. Another condition was that the railway had to be fully constructed within ten years. Because Macdonald had pushed on and forced his vision, Canada would finally have its "steel spine," which would keep the body whole and allow movement within from one coast to the other, thus creating a new Canadian identity.

The actual construction of the railroad was a gigantically monumental endeavour. Geographically, the line had to traverse some of the roughest terrain on the continent: northern Ontario, the Canadian Rocky Mountains, the uneven prairies, and the various tunnels and bridges that needed to be constructed. Politically, the road was rocky as well. Edward Blake, the Liberal leader who had succeeded Alexander Mackenzie, opposed the transcontinental railway; he fought and referred to the scheme as "insanity." During the debate over the Canadian Pacific Railway deal, Blake and his fellow Liberals attempted to capitalize on the complete one-sidedness of the deal by proposing another syndicate—which, as it turned out, had Liberal connections of its own. Macdonald and his government would have none of this bluster.

It was Tupper, though, who began by tearing up the Liberals in the House of Commons. He rose and told those assembled, "We have had tragedy, comedy, and farce from the other side. Sir, it commenced with tragedy. The contract was declared oppressive, and the amount of money to be given was enormous. We were giving away the whole lands of the North-West this was the tragedy.... The comedy was that when every one of the speeches of these honourable gentlemen were read to them, it was proved that last year, or the year before, and in the previous years, they had thought one way, and that now they spoke in another way.... Now, Sir, the last thing that came was the farce. We had the farce laid on the table today. The tragedy and comedy were pretty successful; but the farce, I am afraid, with an impartial audience, in theatrical phrase, will be damned." And damn it he did. He pointed out that the new proposal was created by politicians, not businessmen. Tupper stated that they could use complimentary figures, as they knew that they would not ever have to drive one spike into the ground and therefore could promise anything. Then it was Macdonald's turn. He told the assembled members of Parliament, in striking detail, all of the various flaws in the Liberal scheme. Macdonald, despite suffering from various maladies, told them, "I am not well. But I will be heard." Calling the lightly veiled Liberal syndicate a "farce" and a "political engine," Macdonald was abhorred that the substitute syndicate, which proposed connecting the Canadian Pacific Railway to the American railways, thus bypassing the rough areas in Canada, would destroy "our hopes of being a great nation... we should become a bundle of sticks as we were before, without a binding cord." Macdonald told his fellow parliamentarians, "I can trust to the intelligence of this House, and the patriotism of this country. I can trust not only to the patriotism but to the common sense of this country to carry out an arrangement which will give us all we want, which will satisfy all the loyal, legitimate aspirations, which will give us a great, an united, a rich, an improving, a developing Canada, instead of making us tributary to American laws, to American railways, to American bondage, to American tolls, to American freights, to all the little tricks and big tricks that American railways are addicted to for the purpose of destroying our road."

Despite his ever-increasing ill health, Macdonald knew that he had delivered the speech he needed to give to save the railway. He stated, "I was luckily strong and well when I spoke, which I did in the fashion of twenty years ago." Despite his health and the intense pressure from the Liberals, the Canadian Pacific Bill was finally passed in the House on February 1, 1881. One of the accolades Macdonald received was from a man who had long supported confederation. Alexander Morris, in a letter to Macdonald, wrote, "I write to congratulate you on the second crowning triumph of your more recent life, second only to that of confederation. You have now created the link to bind the provinces indissolubly together, and to give us a future and a British nationality."

John A. Macdonald, 1883.
(Library and Archives Canada, mikan 3218727)

Macdonald had succeeded, yet at a high personal cost to his health. He told Galt, "The long sittings at last broke me down, and I had to betake myself to my bed for a fortnight and am only now beginning to crawl about." So sick was he that he was unable to attend the ceremony whereby the governor general gave royal assent to the bill. After a caucus dinner, the Parliament prorogued on March 21, 1881, and Macdonald suffered a setback. He told Tupper, "There was no ascertainable cause for it, but suddenly I broke down—pulse at forty-nine, and great pain and disturbance in liver and bowels." Macdonald's baffled physician thought he might have "a cancerous affection of the stomach." Despite his misgivings about leaving the party without a leader, and despite giving absolutely no thought to retirement, Macdonald put his personal affairs in order and travelled to England on May 21 to seek medical advice. By mid-July, he was feeling better, and by September, he was on his way back to Canada.

As mentioned earlier, the construction of the Canadian Pacific Railway encountered geographical and political obstacles that delayed its construction. Another major problem was financial. Several times over the course of the construction of the Canadian Pacific Railway, Stephen's financial problems required him to seek monetary help from the prime minister. Unfortunately for Stephen, Macdonald could not unilaterally grant him the desired funds, as he had to go through Parliament for permission to loan money to the railway. Every time they asked for money, the Maritimes and Ontario attempted to extract more concessions from the federal government as recompense for their tax dollars being used for a private venture. On December 15, 1883, Stephen explained to Macdonald that the railway would surely go bankrupt if they did not receive immediate assistance. During a meeting with the Canadian Pacific Railway, Macdonald told Stephen that they might as well ask for the planet Jupiter as expect a loan as large as the one they were asking for. The minister of agriculture, John H. Pope, awoke Macdonald at two a.m. and told him that if the railway failed, then the conservative government would not last twenty-four hours. Faced with this indisputable fact, Macdonald set about to secure the twenty-two-and-a-half-million-dollar loan they required. Parliament realized that, if they did not approve the loan, they would end up paying anyway to finish the railway and then have to manage it. Ultimately, the loan was passed in the House in March 1884. Both the Maritimes and Quebec had secured money from the government to create more railway lines for their areas.

The railway was constructed in three different regions concurrently: British Columbia, northern Ontario, and the Prairies. Workers came to Canada to toil on the railway from China, England, Scotland, and Ireland. Subsequently, because of the adroit leadership of Stephen and his choice of William Van Horne as overseer of construction, the railway was amazingly completed in five years instead of the contractually projected ten years. On November 7, 1885, Donald Smith, Macdonald's one-time political nemesis, drove the last spike at Craigellachie, British Columbia, much to the bruising of Macdonald's pride.

Last Spike of the Canadian Pacific Railway. November 7, 1885. Craigellachie, British Columbia, Canada.
Donald Alexander Smith driving the last spike of the Canadian Pacific Railway. Also in the photo are (left to right): Albert Bowman Rogers (Surveyor), Michael Haney (Contractor), William Cornelius Van Horne (CPR Manager), Sir Sandford Fleming, Edward Mallandaine (teenager), Henry Cambie (Engineer), John Egan (General Superintendent), Sam Steele (NorthWest Mounted Police), James Ross (Engineer). The man at the rear of the photo, just right of centre, with a white cowboy hat and moustache, is reputed to be Tom Wilson, guide & outfitter.
(Wikimedia Commons)

In the summer of 1886, Macdonald, Agnes, and their daughter Mary traveled westward on the newly completed Canadian Pacific Railway. He was finally able to experience the nation he was so instrumental in creating. Aboard their private railway car, the *Jamaica*, the Macdonalds made many stops along the way, to the delight of many. In Winnipeg, several hundred citizens amassed at the station to catch a glimpse of the prime minister. Macdonald waded out into the throngs of people, hat off and hair blowing wildly in the wind. One young observer, a conservative supporter, remarked to a friend in a matter-of-fact fashion, "Seedy-looking old bugger, isn't he?" During a stop at Gleichen, Alberta, hundreds of Blackfoot gathered around the railway siding. Macdonald met Chief Crowfoot, who expressed his loyalty. Crowfoot also pointed out, through an interpreter, that Macdonald's fire-wagons were causing their crops to burn along the railway lines, causing great hardship for his people. Crowfoot also asked Macdonald if he intended to halt the Canadian government's shipments of food, made necessary since the near total annihilation of the buffalo during the construction of the railroad.

Macdonald told Crowfoot he would do his best regarding the fire-wagons. As far as the food shipments were concerned, he stated that the government would be sending seeds for them to grow their own food. Macdonald said, "White men worked hard for their food and clothing and expected Indians to do the same." After an exchange of gifts, the Macdonalds departed and continued their journey westward. A little while later, Agnes, showing the more adventurous side of her personality, decided to venture out onto the train's cowcatcher and enjoy the view from there. She simply stated, "This is lovely," as the train lumbered up to the top of a peak. But then the train began its descent, and despite a mouth full of insects and having to hold on for dear life with all her power, Agnes managed to make it to the bottom. "There was not a yard of that descent in which I faltered for a moment. There [was] glory of brightness and beauty everywhere, and I [laughed] aloud on the cowcatcher, just because it is all so delightful," she reminisced later. After their final stop in Port Moody, British Columbia, the local newspaper, *The Gazette*, reported that "Sir John looks as gay as a lark." A man approached

Macdonald and said that they had met before. Macdonald, with his remarkable memory, stated that they encountered each other at a picnic in Ontario in 1856, "and you may remember it was a rainy day." The man replied, "Yes, that was the very occasion."

From Port Moody, Macdonald and Agnes went on to Vancouver, then to Victoria for a stay of three weeks. MacDonald's personal secretary, Joseph Pope, later reminisced, "As I stood on the shore of the Pacific by the side of that old man, with his grey hair blowing across his forehead, I could not help feeling what an exultant moment it must have been for him. Here was the full realization of his political dream of years. His chief opponent had left on record his belief that all the resources of the British Empire could not build the road in ten years. Here it was built, out of the resources of Canada, in less than half that time. It was no paper road, this. He had travelled over it himself. With his own eyes he had witnessed the marvellous feat. Here was the car which had brought him from Ottawa. Here, too, lapping at his feet were the waters of the Pacific Ocean. His dream had become an accomplished fact!" A short time later, Macdonald and Agnes returned by train to Ottawa.

In 1880, two events helped Macdonald move further toward the Canada we see today. The first was Canada's taking over from Britain the area north of Rupert's land, in the arctic. This created the geographical country as it stands today, without Newfoundland, which would join confederation in 1949. In 1880, Alexander Galt also became Canada's first High Commissioner to England after some negotiations with the British. Despite their deep misgivings about such an office, the British were swayed by Macdonald's argument that they could offer their eyes and ears to the happenings in Washington from their unique position as northern neighbours. The formalization of the relationship with Britain helped begin Canada's long process of foreign relations independence. Macdonald was always fiercely Canadian and protected Canada's interests, even when it did not coincide with Britain's. During the implementation of the National Policy, Macdonald refused to exempt British manufacturers at the expense of other nations, as that would have resulted in trade wars, especially with the economic behemoth to the South. When Britain requested four battalions of Canadian troops for the relief of General Gordon at Khartoum in 1885, despite the public's willingness to partake in the imperial adventure, Macdonald refused the request. Macdonald stated, "Our men and money would be sacrificed to get Gladstone and Co. out of the hole they have plunged themselves into by their own imbecility." Although England still paid to patrol and defend both coasts with the Royal Navy and kept British Regulars garrisoned at various forts within the country, Macdonald felt that Canada had nothing to gain by participating in the follies of empire building. Should the British Isles be threatened, that would be another matter altogether; Canada, with "their strong affection for the mother country, and their desire to maintain the connection," would have unreservedly come to Britain's aid in any fashion required.

During the election of 1882, Macdonald resorted to gerrymandering to help win the election. Representation by population required that, with each census, a redistribution of the seats for Parliament be affected to reflect the new population figures. The 1881 census gave Ontario four more seats, thus allowing for the electoral boundaries to be re-drawn. Macdonald used the situation to "hive the liberals." In essence, the governing conservatives grouped all the strong Liberal towns within small geographical areas into a few seats, thus allowing the other areas to become conservative strongpoints in the majority of seats. The Liberals were aghast at the blatant attempts to move the election in their direction. Macdonald stated wryly to some of his fellow conservatives, "The Grits complain that they are hived all together. It seems they do not like the association—they do not like each other's company. They like to associate with Conservative gentlemen such as you. Your being with them rather gives tone to their society." Despite Macdonald's machinations, and despite their easy win, the Conservatives lost the seats they had expected to win. Macdonald managed to gather enough campaign funds from the beneficiaries of the National Policy and the Canadian Pacific Railway to ensure victory.

By 1883, the Long Depression had resumed its destructive path through the Canadian economy. As they had escaped much of the pain through the last depression, Canada was now experiencing what the United States and the rest of the world had experienced previously. In Canada, general economic malaise struck the country with full force. Commodity prices sank to all-time lows, bank lending became almost non-existent to businesses, unemployment skyrocketed, and many of those lucky enough to retain their jobs had to endure wage cuts. On top of this, provincial-federal relations became much more problematic. In Nova Scotia, the economic hardships caused a resurgence of anti-confederation sentiments. In Ontario, their Premier, Liberal Oliver Mowat, once Macdonald's law student and a Father of Confederation, was vehemently opposed to Macdonald's vision of a strong central government. Although Macdonald often got the upper hand, Mowat proved more than a match for Macdonald; he was able to thwart Macdonald's vision enough to allow the provinces to have more of a voice and slow down the threatening tide of a fierce and potent central government. In Manitoba, there was discontent over high freight rates and subsidies; they agitated for lower rates but were unable to affect any change due to their lack of political and economic power. Meanwhile, there was growing discontent amongst the Plains Aboriginals, whose lifestyle and means of subsistence were decimated during the 1870s and 1880s, with the destruction of the buffalo herds and the creation of restrictive reservations.

Also during this period, there was a large emigration from Canada to the United States. By the turn of the next century, more than one million Canadians were living south of the border. From 1880 to 1900, Canada's population had only grown from four million to five million. To sustain Canada's economic growth, immigrants were needed to fuel the economy. However, many bypassed the nation for the greener pastures of the neighbour to the South. Attempts to settle the Northwest Territories did not yield the expected numbers. By 1900, only about one hundred thousand European Canadians settled there.

During his last decade in power—and indeed the last decade of his life—Macdonald was solely preoccupied with keeping the country together. The Canadian Pacific Railway consumed him for the next few years. After 1882, he placed the most difficult problems on the back burner until they, too, were displaced by more pressing problems. This was his "Old Tomorrow" period, as it became known. Many times throughout his political career, Macdonald put problems off again and again, much to the dismay of those around him. Even he was aware of the nickname. When rumours began circulating of a British peerage, Macdonald, when asked what title he would be likely to take, simply replied: "Lord Tomorrow."

CHAPTER 11
LOUIS RIEL

The greatest troubles for Macdonald and the nation emanated from the West. After the Red River Rebellion of 1869-1870, Louis David Riel, the rebellion's undisputed leader, was sent into exile to the United States. Riel had predicted many people would begin to immigrate to Manitoba, thus forcing the Métis to travel west and settle into the Saskatchewan Valley, along the Southern branch of the North Saskatchewan River around Batoche. The Métis were given, according to the 1870 agreement with the government, a "scrip," or vouchers for free land. Some sold their land to speculators, as suggested by Macdonald; many of the Métis claimed they had never received their allotment of land. All Macdonald was willing to offer them was the one hundred and sixty acres available to all under Canada's homestead policy, instead of the two hundred and forty acres promised under the earlier treaty. Father Alexis Andre, a Roman Catholic priest who worked with the Métis, spoke of their dilemma: "They demanded patents [titles] for their land, demanded frontage on the river, and the abolition of the taxes on wood, and the rights for those who did not have scrip in Manitoba."

By 1884, the buffalo were virtually hunted out of existence. Both Métis and Indigenous peoples were beginning to suffer greatly; the Métis suffered economically, and the Indigenous peoples were starving. For the Métis, the main point of contention was the land claim issue. Despite their protestations to Ottawa, little progress had been made. "Old Tomorrow" hoped that the problem would solve itself before his intervention was required. In March 1884, two dozen South Branch Métis met to discuss the problem. Gabriel Dumont, factional Métis leader and chief, told his fellow Métis at the meeting that they needed to do this for themselves and to "force the government to give us justice." It was agreed that Dumont would lead a delegation of four people, travel six hundred miles to meet Riel in Montana, and attempt to persuade him to return and spearhead their cause.

Gabriel Dumont, 1885.
(Wikimedia Commons)

Riel was living and teaching in Montana with his wife and children. To Riel, teaching was a mundane and unfathomable job. During his many years in the United States, Riel became increasingly more preoccupied with religious matters, rather than political ones. Increasingly beset with mental and physical problems, Riel began to believe he was on a mission from God. In addition to being the divine caretaker of the Métis, Riel also believed himself a prophet and a priest of a brand-new type of Catholicism. In 1875, he received a letter from Bishop Ignace Bourget of Montreal, who told Riel, "I have the deep-seated conviction that you will receive in this life, and sooner than you think, the reward for all your mental sacrifices.... For He has given you a mission which you must fulfill in all respects." Riel had already had a couple of "mystical visions" while in Washington, D.C., during which he shouted and cried during church services. Subsequently, friends with whom Riel had been staying with near Montreal arranged for him to be admitted to an asylum in March of 1876 under the name of Louis R. David, to protect him from his political foes.

During his stay, his physician noted Riel's superior intellect and knowledge of Christian beliefs, Judaism, and classical philosophy. With regards to Riel's theological beliefs, the doctor said, "I never could satisfy myself thoroughly as to whether this sort of talk was not acting a part or an hallucination." After a year and a half—after periodic bouts of clarity, irrationality and violence, and ultimately rest—Riel was discharged with the proviso that he live a quiet and demure life.

Dumont and his three compatriots reached Riel on June 4, 1884. Dumont's party did not include any Indigenous people, nor white settlers from the region from whence they came. After they made their plea for him to return and lead his people, Riel told them that God had sent him a message by sending "four of you who have arrived on the fourth and you wish to leave with a fifth."

Therefore, he decided, "I cannot answer today. You must wait until the fifth." Riel felt that he had finally been given the opportunity to lead his people, a mission foretold by Bishop Bourget ten years earlier. He also pressed Dumont's group on his only other demand: that he be able to pursue his own personal land claim grievance. The terms were accepted, and the group left for home.

Louis Riel, 1883.
(Wikimedia Commons)

Shortly after Riel returned to Batoche, he began to espouse affecting change by acting "orderly and peaceably." Despite all having grievances—the whites wished for responsible government for the territory and representation in Ottawa, the natives detested the reservation and the near-extinction of the buffalo, and the Métis had their land dispute—Riel was never able to meld all three groups into one cohesive voice of opposition to the government. In addition to this, the Indian commissioner and lieutenant governor of the territory, Edward Dewdney, had bribed many of the local newspapers into supporting the government's position and being critical of Riel. Macdonald, at the time, did not take the situation seriously. He stated, "There is, I think, nothing to be feared from Riel." He had "some claims he had against the government. I presume these refer to his land claims which he forfeited on conviction and banishment. I think we shall deal liberally with him and make him a good subject again." At this time, Riel began to mix politics and religion, much to the dismay of Father André and the clergy, who subsequently withdrew their support for Riel. Riel accused Father André of supporting the government, to which André replied that Riel was a "true fanatic" and that he should cease with his constant "heretical and revolutionary ideas." In September of 1884, Bishop Vital-Justin Grandin of St. Albert and Dewdney's personal secretary visited Riel and attempted to bribe him into accepting a seat on the Council of the North-West Territories.

Riel refused the offer; he told the bishop that what he really wanted was the "inauguration of a responsible government," as well as "the same privileges to the old settlers of Manitoba." He also wished for the Métis to have clear titles to their lands, in addition to two hundred and forty acres of land for all mixed-blood people who had not yet received their allotment. The Métis also wanted the proceeds of the sale of two million acres of land to support hospitals, orphanages, and schools, as well as the purchase of ploughs and grain. Riel also demanded that all "works and contracts of the Government of the North-West Territories be given, as far as practicable to residents therein, in order to encourage them as they deserve and to increase circulation of cash in the Territories."

On December 16, 1884, Riel and the committee submitted their petition to the government in Ottawa. With it, they requested that they be able to send a delegation to Ottawa to negotiate "their entry into confederation, with the constitution of a free province." The petition was received by Secretary of State Joseph-Adolphe Chapleau, yet Macdonald, who was Minister of the Interior, denied having ever seen the document.

By February 1885, Riel, after having begun to consider leaving Canada, decided that he would stay. He had yet to receive his two hundred and forty acres, and he owned five lots of land near the Red River. In total, he felt he was owed thirty-five thousand dollars. The government remained ambivalent not only to his claims but the Métis' claims as a whole. When it became apparent that Macdonald was unwilling to consider the Métis land claims, Riel began to pray fanatically as his mental condition progressively worsened. Talk of armed rebellion caused the clergy to remonstrate Riel and his followers against the use of force. The clergy felt that he was preaching his own brand of theology, whereby he renamed the days of the week, made Saturday the Lord's Day, and suggested that Bourget be the new pope and be located in Canada. He also stated that everybody would be priests in his new form of Catholicism. His rejection of Rome caused a great consternation amongst the clergy, which sealed his final break from the church.

During this time, Macdonald and his cabinet were aging and well past their prime. As more and more problems presented themselves, the old guard seemed less able to deal with the problems. Macdonald was seventy years old and often sick. As usual, Macdonald held a plethora of cabinet positions in addition to his duties as prime minister. During this period, he was Minister of the Interior (until 1883), Indian Affairs, the Royal North-West Mounted Police, and in charge of ensuring that the Canadian Pacific Railway reached the Pacific Ocean. Every minute detail within these portfolios passed across Macdonald's desk and needed his personal approval for things to happen. Amid his "Old Tomorrow" phase, Macdonald was totally consumed with the railway, to the almost total exclusion of all his other ministries. Despite the shortcomings and infirmities of his fellow cabinet colleagues, Macdonald soldiered on as best he could. Lord Carnarvon, a British statesman, described Macdonald, during a visit to Canada in 1883, as standing "like Saul, head and shoulders above all his contemporaries and colleagues, and wherever he might be he would have made his mark. His conversation has all the ripened wisdom and perhaps statecraft of an experienced statesman, and his knowledge of affairs in England and of parties there was remarkable. He did not seem strong physically, and said that he felt weary at times of the work, but that his colleagues held him to it, and that several of them said they would not stay if he went."

Macdonald was unaware of Riel's descent into mental instability, but he began in late summer 1884 to hear rumblings of trouble from the West. In August, Macdonald's Public Works Minister travelled to Regina on government business but declined to travel another three hundred and fifty miles to attend a dinner Riel was going to have for him. Riel took the snub as expected; he believed that Macdonald and his government did not view their grievances seriously. Another problem that Macdonald encountered was of his own making. A local judge was instructed to investigate the true nature of the troubles in the area. He reported to Macdonald that all was quiet with the Métis but would not remain so if their land claims were not dealt with expeditiously. He also told Macdonald that the natives were in dire need of food and clothing and that failure to provide those before the winter would cause "great misery and starvation among them during this winter." All Macdonald was willing to do when he came into possession of this report was to dispatch one hundred more members of the North-West Mounted Police to the West. He stated, "I don't apprehend myself any rising, but with these warnings it would be criminal negligence not to take any precautions."

After the government received the Métis petition in December 1884, the government was confused on the matter. The author of the petition, Honoré Jackson, Riel's Caucasian personal secretary, wrote in his covering letter that they wanted the petition sent to "the Privy Council of England... rather than the federal authorities." In the House of Commons in January 1885, Macdonald was asked if he received the petition, to which Macdonald stated, "The Bill of Rights had never been officially or in any way promulgated so far as we know, and transmitted to the government." Macdonald was confusing the petition with a separate Bill of Rights, which Riel never completed.

Honoré Jackson

(Wikimedia Commons)

As soon as he was able, Macdonald acknowledged receipt of the petition. Jackson assumed that meant he and Riel would get a favourable response. Macdonald was leery of allowing the Métis to have the "scrips" because in Manitoba, "The scrip is sold to the sharks and spent in whiskey." Macdonald put the question before his cabinet, and it was subsequently agreed that they would settle the land claim issue as the Métis had wanted. However, Macdonald conveyed a contradictory message to the Métis when he appointed a commission "with a view to settling equitably the claims of half-breeds." When he informed the House on his progress, Macdonald told those gathered that he had acquiesced to allowing a commission "with the greatest reluctance," yet "at the last moment I yielded, and I said 'Well, for God's sake, let them have the scrip; they will either drink it or waste it or sell it, but let us have peace.'" In typical "Old Tomorrow" fashion, though, he did not appoint the commission members until the middle of March.

By the time Riel received the government's response, it had gone through several people before it had arrived at his desk. He was outraged and indignant that the government would try to sidestep him. Riel became more focused on religion and his "mission." Increasingly more erratic, yet still popular with many of his Métis followers, Bishop Grandin feared that Riel had become a "saint" to his people. Father André stated, when speaking about the many confrontations between the clergy and Riel, that "He (Riel) became in those moments truly a maniac, twisting himself into contortions in a rage." André told Riel that, should he persist, the only result would be "war," and that "it would bring down on them all sorts of evils and cover the country with ruin and blood." Riel remained unconvinced, sure that God would protect him and his "mission."

John A. MacDonald

Father Alexis André, 1885. Duck Lake, Saskatchewan.
(Wikimedia Commons)

Father André even went so far as to solicit a promise from Riel to return to Montana, should the government settle his personal land claim. André communicated to Dewdney that "$3,000 to $5,000 would cart the whole (Riel) family across the border," and then Riel "would arrange to make his illiterate and unreasoning followers well satisfied with almost any settlement of their claims for land." MacDonald, remembering that Riel had been paid money to stay out of Canada years earlier, was unimpressed with Riel's gesture and André's plea. Macdonald told the House of Commons that he felt Riel had come to Canada "for the purpose of attempting to extract money from the public purse." And he then added that "Of course that could not be entertained for a moment."

On February 24, 1885, at a meeting in Batoche to discuss the government's decision to create a land claims commission, many in attendance were vocal in their desire that Riel should stay, despite his announcement that he was returning to the United States. At a similar meeting held on March 5, Dumont and ten others signed an undertaking to "save our country from a wicked government by taking up arms." On March 18, after hearing of a report that five hundred North-West Mounted Police were marching in their direction (in reality only fifty Mounted Police and fifty local militia from Fort Carlton were moving toward the South Branch district, with no ulterior motives at that time), Riel and a group of Métis ransacked a number of stores in Batoche with the express purpose of acquiring guns, ammunition, and hostages. After a rebuke from a local priest infuriated him, he declared that "Rome has fallen" and that Bourget would be the new pope. On March 19, Riel declared a provisional government, and he chose fifteen councillors, referred to as the "exovedate," which meant "those picked from the flock." Their first act was to declare that Riel was a "prophet in the service of Jesus Christ." The Exovedate focused almost entirely on religious matters; military matters, according to Riel, were left to God.

Despite Riel's best intentions that there should be no loss of life, that is exactly what happened at Duck Lake on March 26. Dumont and a few hundred Métis converged on Duck Lake and raided a store on March 25. The next day, Dumont's group met a force led by NWMP Superintendent Leif Crozier. After a brief exchange of gunfire, twelve of Crozier's men lay dead, while the Métis lost only five. Despite the victory, Riel decided not to push forward and consolidate his victory.

Instead, he ordered his force back to Batoche, where they remained during the rest of the rebellion. It was the beginning or the end for Riel. First, he had caused bloodshed when he had vowed not to. Second, he did not seize the opportunity to crush his opponents when afforded the opportunity at Duck Lake. He had also expected that Macdonald would not be able to mobilize his forces quickly. That proved to be a miscalculation, as Macdonald could send troops westward in a matter of weeks via the railroad. Finally, Riel never had the support of the English Métis, the whites, or the Indigenous peoples. Had he galvanized his support across the racial and linguistic spectrum, the outcome may have been quite different.

Macdonald was at his shrewdest when it counted, and the North-West Rebellion was no different. With government informants firmly in place in the South Branch region, Macdonald knew five days prior to Duck Lake that armed rebellion was imminent. Macdonald had already begun moving troops and materials westward with great speed, using the railway. With the defeat at Duck Lake, the necessity of moving even more soldiers and North-West Mounted Police westward became much more urgent and truly showed the usefulness of the railway. So, with one broad stroke, Macdonald was able to secure the funding necessary to continue the railway and get his forces into the field at an unheralded pace.

Within three weeks, General Middleton, commander of Canada's forces during the rebellion and a veteran of many of Britain's colonial wars, moved a force of nine hundred men toward Batoche. After some skirmishing and battles—one of which was the Battle of Fish Creek, where two hundred of Riel's Métis, led by Dumont, ambushed and killed ten of Middleton's soldiers and wounded forty-five others before the general and his forces retreated—the Canadian forces finally began moving in earnest toward Batoche. Present at Fish Creek, while preparing for the eventual arrival of the enemy, Riel said, "I have seen the giant; he is coming; he is hideous. It is Goliath." While awaiting Middleton's arrival, religion was the only thing spoken of. Riel confided in his diary, "I pray you to keep away the sons of evil. Stagger them when the fight takes place so ... they will know the Almighty is prepared to inflict retribution upon them."

General Frederick Middleton, 1885.
(Wikimedia Commons)

Middleton finally engaged Riel and his fellow Métis at Batoche on May 9. To no one's surprise, the Canadians won a decisive victory there (the one and only victory of the rebellion they would enjoy). Sorely outnumbered and outgunned, it still came as a huge surprise to Riel that they had lost the battle. To Dumont, he said, "What are we going to do? We are beaten." Dumont replied, "You must have known that in taking up arms we should be beaten."

Dumont fled to the United States. While sitting in the woods outside Batoche, Riel was taken into custody on May 15. He did not even try to escape.

Riel was transported to Regina for his trial; there, under territorial law, a six-man jury was permitted. In Manitoba, the law required a twelve-man jury, and there was a much greater chance that it would be bilingual, unlike in the North-West Territory. Riel was charged with high treason, in addition to five other charges. The trial began on July 20, 1885. Riel pleaded not guilty to all, but from the outset, it was evident that Riel would not escape the hangman's noose. In June, MacDonald said, "If Riel is convicted, he will certainly be executed." Although Riel's lawyers wanted to use a defence of insanity, the defendant insisted throughout the trial that this was not his wish. He knew that his legacy would not withstand such a tactic, and he felt he was not insane. Despite his arguments to his eastern Canadian lawyers, they proceeded using insanity as a defence. He continued to defy them. He stated, "Here I have to defend myself against the accusation of high treason, or I have to consent to the animal life of an asylum. I don't care much about animal life, if I am not allowed to carry with it the moral existence of an intellectual being."

Louis Riel, a prisoner, in the camp of General F.D. Middleton at Batoche. May 16, 1885.

(Wikimedia Commons)

On August 1, 1885, Louis David Riel was found guilty and sentenced to hang. Despite his endless protestations that he was not insane and his often logical rationalizations for his actions, he had committed high treason by inciting a rebellion. Macdonald, always a strong adherent of law and order, based his decision not to intercede and grant clemency on this point alone. There is much debate as to whether the province of Ontario would have abandoned him in the next Election, had he decided to commute Riel's sentence. As for Quebec, when the sentence of hanging was declared and upheld by Macdonald, they felt betrayed and abandoned by the prime minister, even though their own clergy—who, for the most part, yielded considerable sway in Quebec—had not supported Riel, his heretical tendencies, or the armed rebellion that he was leader of. Macdonald could have eased out of the political predicament he was in when the medical commission he summoned after the trial concluded that Riel was sane. As was his way, he could have easily stacked the commission with physicians who, for a price, would have stated and sworn that Riel was a madman and not possibly responsible for his actions.

A RIEL UGLY POSITION.

Protestants demanded Riel be executed; Catholics wanted him to live. The decision for execution alienated Francophones. From Grip magazine. 1885.

(Wikimedia Commons)

Macdonald endured withering attacks from Quebec, who demanded clemency, and from Ontario, who expected Macdonald to cave to Quebec's pressure to save and maintain his government. The wife of John Thompson, Macdonald's Justice Minister, stated, "If you hang him, you make a patriot of him. If you send him to prison, he is only an insane man." Despite the pressure, Macdonald is reported to have said, "He shall hang though every dog in Quebec bark in his favour." Macdonald certainly seemed destined to suffer politically no matter which avenue of action he chose for Riel. In the end, he chose the law, and he stuck to his guns. To his Quebec lieutenant, Hector Langevin, he said, "Keep calm resolute attitude—all will come right.... We are in for lively times in Quebec, but I feel pretty confident that the excitement will die out." How wrong he would turn out to be.

At 8:15 a.m. on November 16, 1885, Louis Riel was led to the gallows by Father André and several other priests, dignitaries, police and soldiers. Just prior to his death, Riel wrote, "I have devoted my life to my country. If it is necessary for the happiness of my country that I should now cease to live, I leave it to the Providence of My God." His final act was to recite the Lord's Prayer with Father André: *Our Father, who art in heaven, Hallowed be thy Name, Thy kingdom come, Thy will be done, in earth as it is in heaven. Give us this day our daily bread; And forgive us our trespasses, As we forgive them that trespass against us; And lead us not into temptation, But deliver us from evil...*

At that moment, Riel dropped to his death. With his death, the Conservative Party in Quebec began its slow descent into irrelevancy. Roman Catholicism in Quebec was undergoing a profound transformation since the midway mark of the nineteenth century. The battle lines were drawn along both theological and political issues. The more liberal of the Catholics supported the Liberal Party both federally and provincially. Then there were those who were moderately conservative and adhered to the separation of church and state and the ultimate supremacy of the latter. Then there were the nationalistic ultra-conservatives who believed that the church held all power over moral issues. The ultra-conservatives—or Castors, as they would become known as—battled with the liberals and the moderate conservatives over "the role of the state in modern society and the place of French-Canadian culture within Canadian federalism."

At the time of Riel's death, the conservatives held provincial power in Quebec. Due to their inaction over the death of Riel, many ultra-conservatives abandoned the party for the liberals. Ultra-nationalist Honoré Mercier became leader of the Quebec Liberal Party, and he defeated the conservatives in the provincial election in early 1887. The split between the two conservative factions would never be healed. By 1896, with Wilfred Laurier's prime ministerial victory, the liberals enjoyed political supremacy in Quebec for much of the twentieth century, thanks to Macdonald's ill-fated decision to not offer a reprieve to Louis Riel in 1885.

Shortly after Riel's hanging, Macdonald went to England for some much-needed rest and recuperation and to consult with his physicians in London. Instead of embarking from Montreal, it was decided that it would be safer for the prime minister to continue by train to Rimouski, where he could board his ship and travel to England. Shortly after he left, a large demonstration was held in Montreal, where dozens of speakers spoke angrily against the "hangman's government" in Ottawa. There, Honoré Mercier, newly elected leader of the provincial Liberal Party, stated that Riel "was a Christian martyr sacrificed to Orange fanaticism." Wilfred Laurier also spoke, stating that if he "had lived on the banks of the Saskatchewan he would have taken up a rifle himself." The wave of nationalism re-awakened in Quebecers had profound repercussions for Canada for the next century.

CHAPTER 12
THE FINAL YEARS

Macdonald felt that the time to retire was upon him. In 1884, he had been lamenting that many of his compatriots from years past were now "like myself, feeble old men," to which someone at the meeting Macdonald was speaking at yelled out, "You'll never die, John A." Despite all his accomplishments, Macdonald knew in his heart that his work was not yet done. As historian Donald Creighton stated, "He had finished the design called Canada. But only the gaunt skeleton of the structure had been raised...." The problems Canada was experiencing were many. The depression continued mercilessly; immigration had slowed to a trickle, thus leaving the western portion of Canada virtually unsettled, while emigration to the United States gathered momentum. French and English Canadians traded barbs back and forth. The Indigenous population languished in the squalor and indignity of the reservation system. The provinces clamoured for more autonomy, while the Americans to the South were still complaining about Canada's continuing policy of arresting American fishing vessels overfishing within Canadian territorial boundaries.

Macdonald also had to worry about his fellow Canadians giving up and joining the American states to the South—a prospect so loathsome and detestable that he seriously considered staying on as prime minister. Macdonald only had to look around and realize that no one possessed his skill, passion, cunning, or sheer will to continue the strenuous heaving and lifting that was required to keep Canada together. He decided to stay and fight another election—an election no one expected him to win. How wrong they were.

Despite the myriad of problems that the nation faced at the time, Macdonald managed to introduce many new and creative ideas that were quite ahead of their time. He gave the native population the franchise without having to forfeit any of their rights. Despite withering attacks by the Liberals, who stated that this measure would "bring a scalping party to the polls," and despite the potential loss of support from many voters, Macdonald pointed out to his detractors that the American slaves who had arrived in Canada using the underground railway had the right to vote, and that no one argued about that. However, the native, he pointed out, "who had formerly owned the whole of this country, were prevented from sitting in the House and from voting for men to represent their interests there."

Macdonald also managed, in 1885, to pass the Franchise Bill, thus giving the federal government full authority over all national elections. Macdonald's ulterior motive here was the large amount of patronage appointments available to fellow conservatives during an election. Also included in the Bill—but later withdrawn—was Macdonald's attempt to give the franchise to women. Macdonald knew that, according to his personal secretary Joseph Pope, women were inherently conservative in their views. Macdonald also pointed out in the House "that Canada should have the honour of first placing woman in the position that she is certain, after centuries of oppression, to obtain ... of completely establishing her equality as a human being and as a member of society with man." Despite the opposition and his withdrawal of the motion, Macdonald was the first national leader in the world to propose granting women the right to vote. Canada was the first nation in the world to debate this issue in its Parliament because of Macdonald.

On January 15, 1887 Macdonald requested that the governor general dissolve Parliament and set an election date of February 22. The odds were stacked heavily against Macdonald, yet liberal leader Edward Blake was unable to capitalize on his golden opportunity to become prime minister. Blake had many issues with which he could have seized upon: the demoralizing effects of the depression, cultural struggles, and according to Creighton, the "sense of national frustration and discouragement." Macdonald was aware of Blake's missed opportunities and used them to his advantage. On February 23, 1887, the conservatives formed the next government with a majority of thirty-seven seats. Macdonald himself had predicted, just prior to election day, in a conversation with the governor general that the conservatives would form a government with a majority of between thirty-five and forty seats.

Despite the problems which existed in Canada at the time, Canadians felt sure enough that Blake was not a suitable person to become prime minister because he was a man whose "manner [was] as devoid of warmth as is a flake of December snow," so they voted for "The Grand Old Man" once more. The Liberals, however, made substantial progress in the province of Quebec, garnering forty-nine percent of the vote. It was not enough though to save Blake from resigning as liberal leader shortly after the election. Macdonald was sorry to see Blake go, as this was the second time he had triumphed over him at the polls. He stated, "I hope he won't resign. We could not have a weaker opponent than he." Wilfred Laurier replaced Blake as liberal leader and immediately set himself to work to create a policy which could defeat Macdonald and his National Policy.

Laurier and his Ontario lieutenant, Sir Richard Cartwright, a bitter enemy of Macdonald's, set about to create a program that would promote North American integration. "Unrestricted Reciprocity" was the liberals' answer to Macdonald's National Policy. Since pro-American feelings were on the rise again as the depression continued unabated, many in Canada were willing to entertain this policy. But as is usually the case, some conservatives began clamouring for a stronger and more resilient economic bond with England. Macdonald would not entertain either policy. He did not object to commercial ties with either the Americans or the British; he just refused to compromise Canadian sovereignty by engaging in a continental union or an imperial federation. Macdonald could easily stifle the conservative motion for imperial federation, but the liberal policy was a tougher nut to crack.

John A. Macdonald, 1890.
(Library and Archives Canada, mikan 3218737)

Cartwright and Laurier advocated a commercial union with the United States, whereby all tariffs would be removed on all products shipped between both countries. This free trade would create a continental economy with a north-south flow of goods, contrary to Macdonald's National Policy, which encouraged an east-west Canadian economic corridor. This free trade proposal, or "Unrestricted Reciprocity" as the Liberals called it, would conceivably create a much larger market for Canada's manufacturers and farmers than ever before, not to mention lower prices for consumers. Macdonald rightfully saw that once economic union with the United States was achieved, it would not be long before annexation was a grim reality. Always a proponent of reciprocity, when it served his and the nation's stated policy objectives,

Macdonald would not accept what Laurier and Cartwright were proposing. By 1891, Laurier felt that Canada had arrived at "a period in the history of this young country where premature dissolution seems to be at hand. What will be the outcome? How long can the present fabric last? Can it last at all?" One newspaper reported, "The Eagle and the beaver would repose together, but the beaver would be inside the Eagle."

Wilfrid Laurier
(Wikimedia Commons)

Macdonald bided his time. He finally felt that the time was right to call an election in January 1891. The vote held on March 5 was fought between Macdonald's National Policy and Laurier's Unrestricted Reciprocity. Macdonald went on the offensive, despite being seventy-six years old, with a vigour unmatched by any of his opponents. Macdonald's election slogan, "The Old Flag, the Old Policy, the Old Leader," was an instant hit with the electorate. The colour poster showed Macdonald being carried on the shoulders of a farmer and a factory worker, holding the red ensign, to great effect. Macdonald was a Canadian patriot who used the concept of loyalty to the nation as a potent emotional weapon during his final election campaign. He stated, "As for myself, my course is clear. A British subject I was born—a British subject I will die. With my utmost effort, with my last breath, will I oppose the 'veiled treason' which attempts by sordid means and mercenary proffers to lure our people from their allegiance." Macdonald later stated outright that, when referring to the Liberals' policy of free trade, "They have as many aliases for their policy as a thief has excuses for his wrong-doing. It has been commercial union, unrestricted reciprocity, and latterly tariff reform; but there is another name by which it must be known, and that is annexation—which is treason."

John A. MacDonald

1891 Canadian election campaign poster for Sir John A. Macdonald.
(Wikimedia Commons)

By 1891, thirty percent of Canadians favoured annexation with the United States. The driving force in the United States was not just the American government but the many businessmen who hoped to gain unfettered access to a new market of five million people. Average Americans were not at all interested in annexing Canada, but President Harrison's Secretary of State, James G. Blaine, from Maine, told his president, "Canada is like an apple on a tree just beyond our reach. Let it alone, and in due time it will fall into our hands." Despite these assertions by the secretary of state, it was common knowledge that the Senate, because of its protectionist proclivities, would have never ratified a free trade agreement with Canada.

Laurier and Cartwright positioned the liberals with a policy which resonated well with the electorate. To counteract the Liberals' policy of Unrestricted Reciprocity, Macdonald began telling the nation's voters that the National Policy was indeed effective, and if it were to end, many Canadian manufacturers would cease to exist, thus causing many thousands of fellow Canadians to lose their jobs. Also, Macdonald pronounced that, as a measure to neutralize the Liberals' policy, Canada would negotiate with the United States to resuscitate the cancelled Reciprocity Treaty, which had created great economic times in the country between 1854 and 1866.

On February 7, 1891, Macdonald penned his last address to the people of Canada. He used the arguments contained in the letter to fight the Liberals on his terms. He stated, "In soliciting at your hands a renewal of the confidence which I have enjoyed, as a Minister of the Crown, for thirty years, it is, I think, convenient that I should take advantage of the occasion to define the attitude of the Government, in which I am First Minister, toward the leading political issues of the day." He told them that since 1878, the economic well-being of Canada was his primary focus. He told them, "Trade was depressed, manufactures languished, and exposed to ruinous competition, Canadians were fast sinking into the position of being mere hewers of wood and drawers of water for the great nation dwelling to the South of us."

He purposely began to drive a wedge between the electorate and the Liberals' unfettered love affair with the United States, through which their instrument of Unrestricted Reciprocity would harken much darker days upon an unsuspecting nation. He continued by stating, "We determined to change this unhappy state of things. We felt that Canada, with its agricultural resources, rich in its fisheries, timber, and mineral wealth, was worthy of a nobler position than that of being a slaughter market for the United States. We said to the Americans: 'We are perfectly willing to trade with you on equal terms. We are desirous of having a fair reciprocity treaty, but we will not consent to open our markets to you while yours remains closed to us.' So we inaugurated the National Policy. You all know what followed. Almost as if by magic, the whole face of the country underwent a change. Stagnation and apathy and gloom—ay, and want and misery too—gave place to activity and enterprise and prosperity."

Macdonald told the nation that because of the National Policy, the country's coffers were "overflowing," and that allowed the government the means with which to "make this country a homogeneous whole." He trumpeted the great achievement that was the Canadian Pacific Railway, the expansion of the canal system, and the lowering of the credit rate which the nation paid on its debt. He reminded people that the Liberals had predicted that the National Policy would be the ruination of the economic health of the country, and that the railway would be a drain on the treasury and would never make money. Then he argued that because all their bold predictions had failed to come true, they invented Unrestricted Reciprocity, and according to Macdonald, "It would, in my opinion, inevitably result in the annexation of this Dominion to the United States." He told the voters that, were free trade to be instituted, "direct taxation" would be the inevitable result. The nation would lose fourteen million in revenue, which would have to be made up somewhere, and that somewhere was off the backs of the common man who could ill-afford to pay it.

He ended by stating:

Gentlemen, this is what Unrestricted Reciprocity involves. Do you like the prospect? This is what we are opposing, and we ask you to condemn by your votes....

The question which you will shortly be called upon to determine resolves itself into this; shall we endanger our possession of the great heritage bequeathed to us by our fathers, and submit ourselves to direct taxation for the privilege of having our tariff fixed at Washington, with a prospect of ultimately becoming a portion of the American Union? I commend these issues to your determination, and to the judgement of the whole people of Canada, with an unclouded confidence that you will proclaim to the world your resolve to show yourselves not unworthy of the proud distinction that you enjoy, of being numbered among the most dutiful and loyal subjects of our beloved Queen.

As for myself, my course is clear. A British subject I was born—a British subject I will die. With my utmost effort, with my latest breath, will I oppose the 'veiled treason' which attempts by sordid means and mercenary proffers to lure our people from their allegiance. During my long public service of nearly half a century, I have been true to my country and its best interests, and I appeal with equal confidence to the men who have trusted me in the past, and to the young hope of the coun-

try, with whom rest its destinies for the future, to give me their united and strenuous aid in this, my last effort, for the unity of the Empire and the preservation of our commercial and political freedom.

I remain, gentlemen, Your faithful servant,

John A. Macdonald

Despite the overwhelming odds against a conservative victory in the election of 1891, Macdonald and his compatriots were victorious over Laurier's Liberal Party. With a majority of twenty-seven seats, with the deciding seats emanating from the Maritime Provinces and the West, and despite the liberals carrying a majority in Ontario and Quebec, Macdonald defeated the pro-American forces once again and kept Canada away from the clutches of the annexationists on both sides of the border. Sir Richard Cartwright, in an infamous bout of of tactlessness, stated that the only reason Macdonald won was because of the "shreds and patches of confederation," which was a direct reference to the Maritimes and Western Canada.

Less than two weeks prior to election day, Macdonald had travelled from Toronto to Kingston for a campaign rally. His pace up to that point was rigorous, to say the least. During the trip, Macdonald was beset with a case of bronchitis, and as they reached Kingston by train, a large storm had struck the area. It was raining when they arrived, and due to the crowded conditions and the warm and acrid atmosphere, when it came time to leave, Macdonald did so at a time when the temperature had plunged dramatically. Pope, his personal secretary, said, "To this sudden change of temperature I attribute the chill, from the effects of which he never fully recovered." After the meeting, Macdonald got into his carriage and told his personal physician, "I never have felt so wearied in all my life." Despite the doctor's order of complete bed rest, Macdonald ventured to Napanee to attend another rally, at the insistence of his many supporters there. Pope wrote that Macdonald: was loath to go, but finally consented; and, on Wednesday the 25th, he started on the fatal trip. The day was raw and bleak. On his arrival at Napanee he was driven in an open carriage to the town hall, where the arrangements for the meeting were very bad. The crowd was so dense that they invaded the platform from which he was speaking. I saw that he was warm and tired and did my utmost to induce the local politicians to allow him to return to his car. Nothing, however, would satisfy them but his presence at another meeting in a different part of town. The open carriage was again called into requisition, and he was driven through the town, where the performance was repeated. When he returned to the car there were several telegrams awaiting him. I went to his room to take his instructions, and found him lying across the bed, his face of an ashen grey. 'I am exhausted,' he said, and indeed he looked it.

Pope immediately cancelled the rest of Macdonald's engagements, and he retired to bed at the home of his brother-in-law, James Wilkinson. On March 4, Macdonald left for Ottawa and immediately retired to his bed at his home, Earnscliffe, where he remained throughout March and April. Unlike previous bouts of illness and exhaustion, this time, according to Pope, when Macdonald became mobile in early May, "I (Pope) first became seriously alarmed. He did not seem to gain strength and complained again and again of feeling weak. His colour, too, was bad; that ashen hue of which I have spoken being often on his face, especially at the close of a long day's work."

On April 29, 1891, Parliament opened. Macdonald had the

pleasure of taking the member's oath with his son Hugh John, who was now a lawyer and newly elected MP from Manitoba. They "together fixed their autographs to the parchment, the son signing on the line below Sir John." He then entered the House of Commons "arm in arm" with his son, a proud moment for the "Grand Old Man". One observer stated, "The old chief never looked better. He was dressed in a frock coat with light trousers, with the traditional red necktie and 'stovepipe' hat. His eye was clear, his step elastic, and everything betokened that he was in good condition for the hard work of the session." When debate began after the Throne Speech, Macdonald taunted Laurier on his electoral defeat. He stated to the House, "I tell my friends and I tell my foes: *J'y suis, j'y reste*. We are going to stay here, and it will take more than the power of the honourable gentleman, with all the phalanx behind him, to disturb us or to shove us from our pedestal." Telling Laurier, "I am here, I am staying here," was the only time Macdonald ever spoke French in the House of Commons.

Macdonald was still terribly weak and ill, and everyone around him and in the House of Commons knew it. On May 12, he ventured to the Commons for a meeting with the governor general and John Thompson regarding the Bering Sea fisheries dispute with the Americans. Pope was there, and he "noticed at the time that there was something wrong with his speech." Immediately, Macdonald told Pope that Thompson "must come at once, because he must speak to the Governor for me, as I cannot talk. There is something wrong with my speech." After the meeting, the governor general and Thompson discussed Macdonald's condition. After they left, Macdonald sought out Pope. His private secretary stated, "For the first time in my life, I noticed a trace of nervousness in his manner. 'I am afraid of paralysis,' he said; 'both my parents died of it,' and, he added slowly, 'I seem to feel it creeping over me.'" Macdonald had also spoken of weakness in his left arm and tingling in his left hand and fingers. Despite this, he told Pope, "You must be careful not to mention this to Lady Macdonald."

Although most of the symptoms of his stroke had ceased by that evening, Macdonald, still weak, continued with his Parliamentary duties. Social duties were not forgotten either. He insisted that he and Agnes host their regular Saturday evening dinner for his caucus. Macdonald managed to get through the dinners on May 16 and 23 with little outward difficulty.

However, at the end of each event, he collapsed into bed, thoroughly exhausted. On May 28, after an evening of work with Pope, at 2:30 a.m., Agnes was awoken by her husband yelling. As she attended to him, he confessed to her that he had lost all feeling in his left leg. By mid-afternoon, the symptoms of Macdonald's second stroke had dissipated, and he could still speak. After the doctors and his wife left his room, Macdonald instructed Pope to bring him his estate papers, stating, "I will sign now while there is time."

At four o'clock on May 29, while being examined by his doctor, Macdonald "gently leaned his head back on the pillow, yawned once or twice, and became apparently unconscious." From the third stroke, Macdonald did not recover. His wife Agnes, his son Hugh, and his daughter Mary were by his side for the next eight days. The conservative ministers and caucus, all members of the House of Commons, and indeed the nation were dumbfounded when they heard that their prime minister was on his deathbed. Pope stated:

The history of Sir John's last illness is in some respects an epitome of his life. As long as he could he strove against the sense of weariness that oppressed him, and when at length the inexorable laws of nature asserted their sway, he assumed that quiet dignity which ever marked his acceptance of the inevitable, and calmly awaited the last dread summons.

Macdonald languished for days after his third stroke. As had become the custom, many members of the newspaper trade were camped outside Macdonald's home, Earnscliffe. It was the habit of the doctors to post updates on the health of Macdonald at irregular intervals. On June 4, the latest bulletin stated, "Sir John MacDonald passed a fairly comfortable night.... His cerebral symptoms are slightly improved at the time of our consultation...." At two p.m. the next day, the doctor's bulletin stated, "At a consultation today we find Sir John Macdonald altogether in a somewhat alarming state. His strength, which has gradually failed him during the past week, shows a marked decline since yesterday.... In our opinion his powers of life are steadily waning."

At 10:24 p.m. on Saturday, June 6, 1891, Joseph Pope exited Earnscliffe and walked toward the gate at the front of the property, where the newspapermen congregated, waiting for the latest report. By that time, there were only a couple or reporters in attendance. When Pope arrived, he simply stated, "Gentlemen, Sir John Macdonald is dead. He died at a quarter past ten." Pope affixed the bulletin to the gate and retired inside.

Within an hour, the news had spread across the whole nation. The entire country grieved for the man who was so instrumental in the creation of Canada and who had worked tirelessly for nearly twenty-five more years to keep the nation together. Tributes and condolences poured in almost immediately to Agnes, Mary, and Hugh at Earnscliffe. Queen Victoria sent a telegram to the governor general, stating, "I am deeply grieved at the news of the death of Sir John Macdonald. He will be a great loss to Canada and to his Sovereign. Pray express my deep sympathy with Lady Macdonald." In the House of Commons two days later, Hector-Louis Langevin, Macdonald's senior Quebec lieutenant, stated,

"My heart is full of tears. I cannot proceed." Wilfred Laurier, Macdonald's defeated opponent in the last election, rose and stated, "In fact, the place of Sir John A. Macdonald in this country was so large and so absorbing that it is almost impossible to conceive that the politics of this country, the fate of this country, will continue without him. His loss overwhelms us."

On Sunday, June 7, Macdonald's body was dressed in his Privy Councillor uniform and placed in a mahogany casket in the dining room of his home. That afternoon, many friends and relatives visited and paid their respects to Agnes, Mary, and Hugh. On the morning of June 9, a private funeral service was given at their home, and late in the afternoon, Macdonald lay in state in the Senate Chamber at the Parliament Buildings. Many thousands of Canadians viewed his body and paid their last respects. From there, he was taken to St. Albans Church, and after the service, he was taken to the railway station, where his body would travel for his burial in Kingston. In his will, Macdonald stated, "I desire that I shall be buried in the Kingston cemetery near the grave of my mother, as I promised her that I should be there buried."

Funeral of Sir John A. Macdonald in Cataraqui Cemetery, Kingston, Ontario. June 1891.

(Wikimedia Commons)

Sir John A. Macdonald was buried in Cataraqui Cemetery, near the bodies of his mother and father; his two sisters, Margaret and Louisa; his brother, James Shaw; and possibly his infant son, John Alexander. And in the end, Sir John A. Macdonald, who was born a British subject, died a British subject—with a Canadian heart.

BIBLIOGRAPHY

1. Beal, Bob, and Rod Macleod. *Prairie Fire: The 1885 North-West Rebellion*. Edmonton: Hurtig; 1984
2. Berton, Pierre. *The Last Spike*. Toronto: Anchor Canada, 1971 (2001 edition)
3. Berton, Pierre. *The National Dream: The Great Railway, 1871-1881*. Toronto: Anchor Canada, 1970 (2001 edition)
4. Biggar, E.B. *Anecdotal Life of Sir John Macdonald*. Montreal: Lovell, 1891.
5. Bliss, Michael. *Right Honourable Men: The Descent of Canadian Politics from Macdonald to Chretien*. Toronto: Harper Perennial Canada, 2004.
6. Bowering, George. *Egotists and Aristocrats: the Prime Ministers of Canada*. Toronto: Viking, 1999.
7. Boyden, Joseph. *Louis Riel and Gabriel Dumont*. Toronto : Penguin Canada, 2010.
8. Burt, A.L. "Peter Mitchell on John A. Macdonald" CHR 42, no. 3 (1961)
9. Collins, Joseph Edmund. *Life and Times of the Rt. Hon. Sir John A. Macdonald, Premier of the Dominion of Canada*. London: Rose, 1883.
10. Creighton, Donald G. *John A. Macdonald. Vol.1, The Young Politician*. Toronto: Macmillan, 1952.
11. Creighton, Donald G. *John A. Macdonald. Vol.2, The Old Chieftan*. Toronto: Macmillan, 1955.
12. Creighton, Donald G. *John A. Macdonald, Confederation and the West*. Winnipeg: Manitoba Historical Society, 1967.

13. Daschuk, James. *Clearing the Plains: Disease, Politics of Starvation, and the Loss of Indigenous Life*. Regina: University of Regina Press, 2019.
14. Donaldson, Gordon. *The Prime Ministers of Canada*. Toronto: Doubleday Canada, 1994.
15. Dutil, Patrice & Hall, Roger. *Macdonald at 200: New Reflections and Legacies*. Toronto: Dundurn, 2014.
16. Ewart, John S. *Sir John A. Macdonald and the Canadian Flag*. Toronto: 1908.
17. Flanagan, Thomas. *Riel and Rebellion: 1885 Reconsidered*. Saskatoon: Western Producer Books, 1983
18. Friesen, Gerald. "Prairie Indians, 1840-1900: The End of Autonomy." *In The Challenge of Modernity: A Reader in Post- Confederation Canada*, edited by Ian McKay. Toronto: McGraw-Hill Ryerson, 1992.
19. Gibson,Sarah Katharine and Arthur Milnes, eds. *Canada Transformed: The Speeches of John A. Macdonald*. Toronto: McClelland & Stewart, 2014
20. Grenville, John. "In Memoriam: Kingston Mourns Sir John A. Macdonald" *Historic Kingston* 40 (1992)
21. Gwyn, Richard. *John A: The Man Who Made Us, The Life and Times of John A. Macdonald, Vol 1,: 1815-1867*. Toronto: Vintage Canada, 2008.
22. Gwyn, Richard. *Sir John A. Macdonald: His Life, Our Times, Vol 2,: 1867-1891*. Toronto: Vintage Canada, 2012.
23. Johnson, J. K. and P. B. Waite, "MACDONALD, Sir JOHN ALEXANDER," in *Dictionary of Canadian Biography*, vol. 12, University of Toronto/Université Laval, 2003–, accessed March 11, 2021, http://www.biographi.ca/en/bio/macdonald_john_alexander_12E.html.
24. Larmour, Jean, B.D. "Edgar Dewdney and the

Aftermath of the Rebellion," *Saskatchewan History* (1970)

25. Leighton, Douglas. "A Victorian Civil Servant at Work: Lawrence Vankoughnet and the Caanadian Indian Department, 1874-1893." In *As Long As the Sun Shines and Water Flows*, edited by Ian Getty and Antoine Lussier. Vancouver: UBC Press, 1983.

26. Macpherson, J. Pennington. *Life of the Right Hon. Sir John A. Macdonald*. Saint John, N.B.: Earle Publishing House, 1891.

27. Martin, Ged. *Favorite Son: John A. Macdonald and the Voters of Kingston, 1841-1891*. Kingston: Kingston Historical Society, 2010.

28. Martin, Ged. *John A. Macdonald: Canada's First Prime Minister*. Toronto: Dundurn, 2013.

29. Morton, Desmond. *The Last War Drum: The North West Campaign of 1885*. Toronto: Hakkert, 1972.

30. Phenix, Patricia. *Private Demons: The Tragic Personal Life of John A. Macdonald*. Toronto: McClelland & Stewart, 2006.

31. Pope, Joseph. *Memoirs of the Rt. Hon. Sir John A. Macdonald, G.C.B., First Prime of the Dominion of Canada*. Ottawa: J. Durie and Son, 1894.

32. Pope, Maurice. *Public Servant: The Memoirs of Sir Joseph Pope*. Toronto: Oxford University Press, 1960.

33. Reynold, Louise. *Agnes: The Biography of Lady Macdonald*. [Toronto: Samuel Stevens, 1979]; Montreal and Kingston: McGill-Queen's University Press, 1990.

34. Smith, Cynthia M., and Jack McLeod, eds. *Sir John A.: An Anecdotal Life of Sir John A. Macdonald*. Toronto: Oxford University Press, 1989.

35. Smith, Donald. "John A. Macdonald and Aboriginal Canada" *Historic Kingston 50* (2002)
36. Smith, Donald. "Macdonald's Relationship with Aboriginal Peoples", In *Macdonald at 200: New Reflections and Legacies.* Dutil, Patrice & Hall, Roger, eds. Toronto: Dundurn, 2014.
37. Stonechild, Blair and Bill Waiser. *Loyal Till Death: Indians and the North-West Rebellion.* Calgary: Fifth House, 1997
38. Swainson, Donald. *Sir John A. Macdonald: The Man and the Politician.* 2nd ed. Kingston: Quarry Press, 1989.
39. Teatero, William "BRASS, WILLIAM," in *Dictionary of Canadian Biography*, vol. 7, University of Toronto/Université Laval, 2003–, accessed May 30, 2021, http://www.biographi.ca/en/bio/brass_william_7E.html
40. Thomas, Lewis H. "RIEL, LOUIS (1844-85)," in *Dictionary of Canadian Biography*, vol. 11, University of Toronto/Université Laval, 2003–, accessed May 10, 2021, http://www.biographi.ca/en/bio/riel_louis_1844_85_11E.html.
41. Tobias, John L. "Canada's Subjugation of the Plains Cree, 1879-1887" *CHR* 64, no.4 (1983).
42. Waite, Peter. *John A. Macdonald.* Toronto: Fitzhenry & Whiteside, 1976.
43. Wallace, C. M. "SMITH, Sir ALBERT JAMES," in *Dictionary of Canadian Biography*, vol. 11, University of Toronto/Université Laval, 2003–, accessed May 30, 2021, http://www.biographi.ca/en/bio/smith_albert_james_11E.html.
44. Whelan, Edward. *The Union of the British Provinces, a*

Brief Account of the Several Conferences Held in the Maritime Provinces and in Canada, in September and October 1864, on the Proposed Confederation of the Provinces. Charlottetown, 1865.

www.ingramcontent.com/pod-product-compliance
Lightning Source LLC
Chambersburg PA
CBHW010447010526
44118CB00021B/2530